WORLD WAR II
An Illustrated Miscellany

A British Bren Gun team practises during the opening weeks of the war

WORLD WAR II
An Illustrated Miscellany

ANTHONY A. EVANS

OTTAKAR'S
2005

CONTENTS

First published in Great Britain in 2005
by Ottakar's Plc, Brewery House
36 Milford Street, Salisbury
Wiltshire SP12AP

Copyright © Worth Press Ltd, 2005
23 Prospero Road, Upper Holloway,
London N19 3QX

ISBN 1 84567681 5

A CIP catalogue record for this book
is available from the British Library

Compiled and designed for Ottakar's Plc
by Worth Press Ltd
Designed and edited by
DAG Publications Ltd, London.
Compiled by Anthony A. Evans.
War Timeline by David Gibbons

Printed and bound in Singapore by Imago

Illustrations are reproduced by courtesy of
the US National Archives, US Department of
Defense, *Illustrated London News*, *Signal*, PageantPix
and the author's collection. While every effort has
been made to trace and acknowledge all copyright
holders, the publishers would like to apologise
should there be any errors or omissions

Towards World War II

The seeds of World War II were sown in the aftermath of World War I. The peace treaty altered many borders, dismembered the Austro-Hungarian and Turkish Empires, and created new states. Germany lost territory and its colonies, suffered under a heavy indemnity imposed by the victors, and faced severe restrictions upon her armed forces. During the 1920s, Germany seethed with resentment at these measures; social unrest was rife and the economy collapsed. Public opinion polarised between Communists and right-wing Nationalists, who fought out their differences on the streets. Several coup attempts failed. One of these, on November 9, 1923 in Munich, was led by an ex-soldier, Adolf Hitler. The putsch failed and Hitler was imprisoned for nine months, during which time he wrote his political manifesto, Mein Kampf.

In Italy, meanwhile, a coup did succeed. The Fascist Party led by Benito Mussolini seized power in October 1922. Impelled by grandiose ambitions, he embarked upon a campaign of conquest in Africa, invading and conquering Abyssinia in 1935–36. World opinion was outraged, but international action against the aggressor was limited.

By 1932 Hitler's political party, the National Socialists (Nazis), had become the largest party in the German Reichstag, after much violence and street fighting. On January 30, 1933 after a political impasse, Hitler became Chancellor of Germany. On March 23, 1933 the parliament granted him powers allowing him to rule by decree, and Germany became a one-party, Nazi state. When President von Hindenburg died, Hitler combined the roles of president and chancellor, naming himself 'Führer'.

In March 1936 Hitler began to implement his programme to reassert Germany's position in the world, sending troops to take control of the Rhineland, occupied by the Allies since World War I. And, two years later, he achieved his aim of uniting the two German-speaking nations of Europe by annexing Austria (the Anschluss).

The lessons of Abyssinia were not lost on Hitler. Western democracies were weak in their response to aggressive expansionism, all too aware of a public opinion that appeared willing to countenance any humiliation rather than face another terrible war. At Munich, they caved in over Hitler's demands to incorporate the German-speaking area of Czechoslovakia (Sudetenland) into Germany.

The sticking-point, however, came with Poland. In October 1938 Hitler demanded the restoration of Danzig to Germany and communications rights in the 'Danzig Corridor' of Polish territory that separated Germany and the province of East Prussia. The Poles refused. At last standing up to Hitler, Britain and France publicly stated their support for Poland, and when, in September 1939, Hitler invaded that country, they issued an ultimatum to Germany that resulted in world war.

On the far side of the world, another ruthless dictatorship was set to take advantage of the Europeans' preoccupations. Following conquests in the Russo-Japanese War and subsequently, and with an alarmingly fast-growing population, Japan had become increasingly expansionist after World War I. In 1931 Japan conquered Manchuria, and six years later invaded China.

By 1940 German conquests in Europe had weakened the position of the European imperial powers in the Far East. Japan coerced the Vichy French to permit Japanese troops to enter Indo-China, from where Japan could interdict the Burma Road, the route used by the USA to supply the Chinese. On July 26, 1941, following unproductive negotiations, the USA froze Japanese assets in America, and Japan finalised her plans for war.

1939

AUGUST SEPTEMBER OCTOBER NOVEMBER DECEMB

● **Sept 4** British aircraft make first attack of the war on German coast near entrance to the Kiel Canal. It is not successful and 7 aircraft are lost

Dec 18 ●
Disastrous RAF daylight bombing attack on the Schillig Roads; 12 of 24 bombers are lost

● **Oct 16** German aircraft open hostilities against the British Isl raiding the Firth of Forth and damaging the cruisers *Edinburgh Southampton*

GERMAN CONQUEST OF POLAND

RUSSO-FINNISH

Sept 1 ●
Germany invades Poland

● **Sept 12** Battle of the River Bzura: Polish Poznan Army attempts to break out of its encirclement. The offensive fails by the 18th; 170,000 surrender

Nov 30 ●
Soviet troops invade Finland, having broken off diplomatic relations the previous day. They attack up the Karelian Isthmus. They are held by the Finnish defences, the Mannerheim Line

● **Dec 3** Finnish forces pull back behind the Mannerheim Lir defences which stretch across th isthmus

Sept 17 ●
Soviet armies invade Poland from the east

● **Sept 27** Warsaw surrenders

Sept 15 ●
German armies surround Warsaw

● **Sept 28** Modlin area: 10 Polish divisions, encircled for 18 days, surrender

● **Dec 6** Sovie attacks agains Mannerheim L begin. These c later attempts

● **Sept 19** Meeting of German and Soviet invading armies at Brest-Litovsk

Nov 30 to Jan 8 B of Suomussalmi. S attacking forces or central front are surrounded and destroyed by the F blizzard conditions temperatures of –4 27,000 Russians ar killed or freeze to c 50 tanks are destro

Aug 23 ●
Non-Aggression Pact signed by Germany and the Soviet Union

Sept 22 ●
Soviet troops take Lvov

● **Oct 6** End of Polish resistance

● **Sept 30** General Sikorski forms Polish government-in-exile in Paris

● **Sept 9** British Expeditionary Force begins crossing to France

Sept 2 Britain and France issue an ultimatum to Germany: withdraw from Poland within 12 hours
Sept 3 No response is forthcoming from Germany. Britain and France declare war on Germany
Sept 5 USA declares its neutrality
Sept 6 South Africa declares war on Germany
Sept 10 Canada declares war on Germany

● **Nov 8** Attempt to assassinate Hitler in Munich fails

Dec 14 ●
Russia expelled from the League of Nations

Aug 25 ●
Formal alliance signed by Poland and Britain

● **Sept 3** British liner *Athenia* sunk by U-30, the U-boat captain believing his target to be an auxiliary cruiser. 28 Americans are among the dead. Britain sees this as the start of unrestricted submarine warfare by the Germans and instigates a system of convoys

● **Oct 14** U-boat U-47 enters the supposedly secure British fleet anchorage of Scapa Flow and sinks the battleship *Royal Oak* with the loss of over 800 crew. The U-boat returns to Germany, and the commander, Leutnant Günther Prien, and crew are fêted

Dec 13 Batt of the River Pl British cruisers *E Ajax* and *Achille Graf Spee* and a hour gun batt ensues, the he armament of t German ship infl damage on two e British. *Graf Spee* into the neutr Uruguayan por Montevideo for re while British reinforcemen concentrate. Be they arrive, how the German Cap Langsdorff is bl into thinking him trapped in the R Plate. On Dec 1 scuttles his ship commits suici

German commerce raiders *Deutschland* and *Admiral Graf Spee*, both 'pocket battleships', are already at sea and awaiting activation upon the outbreak of war. *Deutschland* is in the North Atlantic; *Graf Spee* is in the South Atlantic. There are also 16 of Germany's 57 U-boats at sea

Sept/Oct
Germans lay magnetic mines in British coastal shipping lanes

● **Sept 17** British aircraft carrier *Courageous* sunk by German U-boat U-29 south-west of Ireland. The submarine is sunk by the carrier's escorting destroyers

Nov 21–7
First North Atlantic commerce-raiding cruise by German battlecruisers *Scharnhorst* and *Gneisenau*

Nov 23 ●
British auxiliary cruiser (armed liner) *Rawalpindi* sunk defending convoy against *Scharnhorst* and *Gneisenau*

British naval forces are deployed to the South Atlantic in search of *Graf Spee*

1940

● **March 16**
Scapa Flow
bombed

● **April 11**
Stavanger bombed

● **May
15/16** Ruhr
bombed

● **March 19/20**
Sylt bombed

GERMAN CONQUEST
OF NORWAY AND DENMARK
Naval battles: see below

● **April 30**
Andalsnes
bridgehead
evacuated

May 28 ●
Allies
capture
Narvik

O-FINNISH WAR

an 8 Finns
ke another
ccessful
unterattack,
s time on
central
nt

an 7 Stalin
oints
oshenko to
mand Soviet
es in Finland.
egroups and
forces
aratory to a
wed major
nsive

● **Feb 1** Timoshenko
launches a major
attack across Viipuri
Bay, which is covered
by ice, attempting to
outflank the
Mannerheim Line

● **Feb 11–13**
Mannerheim Line
breached. Finns
withdraw to a second
line of defence

Feb 28–29 Soviets
break through the
Finnish second line
of defence

● **March 8**
Viipuri falls

● **March
12** Peace
signed
in Moscow

April 9
Germany
invades
Denmark and
Norway

April 15 ●
British forces
land near
Narvik

● **April 9** Germans take Copenhagen

April 15 ●
British forces
land near
Narvik

● **April 24** French troops
reinforce the Andalsnes
bridgehead

● **April 18** A third British force
lands at Andalsnes

April 9 ●
German cruiser
Blücher sunk by
coastal guns in
Oslo Fjord

● **April 16** British and French
forces land at Namsos

May 2 Namsos
bridgehead evacuated

March 3 ●
Huge Soviet attack on the
southern front

March 20 ●
Reynaud replaces Daladier as Prime Minister
of France. He promises Britain not to make a
separate peace with Germany

BLITZKRIEG IN
THE WEST

May 10 ●
Germany invades the
Netherlands and Belgium

● **May 13**
Germans
cross Meuse
near Sedan

May 10 ●
BEF and 3 French armies enter Belgium

● **May 15**
Germans
break out of
Meuse/
Sedan
bridgehead

May 10 ●
German paratroops secure the Eben Emael
fortress, key to the defence of Liège

● **Feb 5** Britain and France
plan to send an expeditionary
force to aid the Finns, but on
23rd Sweden refuses to allow
troops to cross the country

Spring/early summer
Lull in the Battle of the
Atlantic as U-boats are
redeployed to Norway

British counterattack at Arras fails **May 21** ●

Germans enter Brussels **May 17** ●

May 20 ●
Germans reach the mouth of the River
Somme and split the Allies in two

sh, British and French
tanalysts penetrate the
twaffe's 'Red' Enigma
codes until May

March 31/April 1 ●
Atlantis is first of the German auxiliary
cruisers (raiders disguised as
merchantmen) to set out; *Orion* follows
six days later

May 23 ●
Panzers halt to regroup, having cut off the
BEF, French First Army and Belgian Army

May 14
Germans bomb Rotterdam

May 27 ●
Germans
take
Calais

April 5–8 ●
Britain and France begin mining Norwegian
waters (Operation 'Wilfred') in order to
interdict the shipping of iron ore from
northern Sweden to Germany

May 14 ●
Dutch Queen Wilhelmina
and government evacuate
to London

● **May 15**
Surrender
of the
Netherlands

April 9 ●
German battlecruisers *Scharnhorst* and *Gneisenau* encounter
British battlecruiser *Renown* off Lofoten Islands. *Gneisenau*
sustains damage before the German units escape

● **April 10** First
Battle of Narvik
Fjord: in a destroyer
action, each side
loses two ships

● **May 10**
Winston Churchill
becomes Prime
Minister of Britain

Feb 16 ●
British destroyer *Cossack* enters
Norwegian waters to rescue
British prisoners taken by *Graf
ee* from the raider's supply ship
Altmark. This is a violation of
orway's neutrality by both sides

April 8 ●
Off Trondheim, Norway, the British
destroyer *Glowworm* encounters part of
the forces already at sea to support the
German invasion of Norway. Massively
outgunned, *Glowworm* rams the cruiser
Admiral Hipper before being sunk

● **April 13** Second Battle of Narvik
Fjord: British destroyers and battleship
Warspite sink 7 German destroyers

1940

JUNE	JULY	AUGUST	SEPTEMBER	OCTOBE

● **June 11** Italians begin bombing Malta

● **July 1/2** Kiel bombed (first RAF use of 2,000lb bomb, on *Scharnhorst*)

BATTLE OF BRITAIN AND 'THE BLITZ'

● **July 10 to Aug 12** ●
The preparatory phase of the Battle of Britain is characterised by relatively small-scale attacks on shipping and night-time aerial mining of the coastal shipping lanes. Losses: Luftwaffe 261, RAF 127

Aug 13 ● Adlertag ('Eagle Day'), official German opening of the Battle of Britain, postponed from 9th. Luftwaffe flies nearly 1,500 sorties in 24 hours

● **Aug 15** Heaviest dogfights thus far. Losses: Luftwaffe 79, RAF 34

● **Sept 7** Turning-point of the Battle of Britain: Luftwaffe changes strategy to all-out assault on London

● **Sept 30** London Yeovil (Westland A factory) raids repe Losses: Luftwaffe RAF 18. This sees last of the large d raids; Germany sv to night bombing

Aug 18 ● Heavy attacks on RAF airfields. Losses: Luftwaffe 69, RAF 39

● **Aug 18** Heavy attacks on RAF airfields. Losses: Luftwaffe 69, RAF 39

Oct 1 to Nov 1 night (excl 6th) L suffers a bombing an average of aircraft.

● **June 3–8** Allies evacuate remaining forces from Norway; King Haakon goes with them

● **June 24/5** British Commandos make their first raid, on the coast of France

Aug 13 to Sept 6
Central phase of the Battle of Britain as Luftwaffe attacks RAF airfields. RAF increasingly suffers a shortage of pilots. Losses: Luftwaffe 629, RAF 385

● **Sept 15** Göring sends in a massive series of attacks on London, marking the climax o battle. This day is commemor in Britain as 'Battle of Britain Losses: Luftwaffe 56, RAF 29

Aug 25/26 ●
RAF bombs Berlin in response to German accidental bombing of London the previous night

The Germans now see that they have not achieved the air supremacy over Britain necessary for the invasion; on 17th Hitler postpones the operation indefinitely and on Oct 12 abandons it

● **O** Over bomb Lond

BELGIUM, FRANCE, NETHERLANDS

Aug 4–17
Italians invade British Somaliland

E Poor weather hampers operations a Battle of Britain is over. Raids on Britain's continue into spring 1941, building to a in May before Luftwaffe units are trans east for the invasion of the

● **June 12** 51st Highland Division and 4 French divisions surrender between Dieppe and Le Havre

● **June 30/July 1** Germany occupies Channel Islands

● **July 23** British Local Defence Volunteers, established on May 14, becomes the Home Guard

May 28 Belgium surrenders

● **June 12** Germans take Paris

NORTH AFRICA

May 17 De Gaulle's French 4th Armoured Division counterattacks unsuccessfully near Laon

● **July 22** Establishment of SOE, Special Operations Executive, to foment resistance in Nazi-occupied Europe

Sept 13 ● Italians invade Egypt

● **Sept 16** Italians take Sidi Barrani and fortify it

● **June 6** Germans reach River Aisne

● **June 22** Franco-German armistice

Aug 8 ●
First *bombe* developed by Alan Turing at Bletchley Park becomes operational and can read 'Red' Enigma again

● **Sept 3** Vienna Award: Germany forces Romania to cede Transylvania to Hungary. The Romanian government collapses and King Carol II abdicates. Power is seized by pro-Nazi General Ion Antonescu

● **Sept 24** Major reint ments arrive in Egypt

May 26 to June 4 Evacuation of trapped Allied troops from Dunkirk

● **June 28** De Gaulle is recognised by Britain as leader of the Free French

● **July 3** Concerned with the possibility of the French Navy falling into German hands, Britain seizes all French ships in British ports

● **Sept 27** Tripartite pact by Germany, Ita and Japan: the Axis powers will support another in the event attack

● **June 4** Germans take Dunkirk

● **June 5** Germans attack south

● **June 20** Italy invades France

● **July 3** At Oran / Mers-el-Kébir British demands that French naval units there join Britain or be demobilized are met with defiance. The British open fire, sinking the battleship *Bretagne* and damaging two others

THE DAKAR EXPEDITION

● **Sept 23–25** A nave force ignominiously fe persuade the French African colony to ren its loyalty to Vichy

June 24 ●
Armistice between France and Italy

● **July 7** Admiral Godefroy at Alexandria with the battleship *Lorraine*, 3 heavy cruisers, 1 light cruiser, 3 destroyers and a submarine agrees to demobilise his ships

● **Sept 7** Britain is on highest alert ('Cromwell') for invasion; it lasts 12 days

June 10 Italy enters the war

● **July 7/8** An ultimatum to French ships at Dakar is rebuffed. The battleship *Richelieu* is attacked by small craft and damaged by an aerial torpedo from the carrier *Hermes*

● **Sept 6** First 8 Lend-Lease destroyers handed over by USA to Britain

Oct German p battleship A *Scheer* b anti-commerce

● **June 8** German battlecruisers *Scharnhorst* and *Gneisenau* encounter British carrier *Glorious* returning from Norway; she and two escorting destroyers are sunk

BLITZ'

- **Mid-Nov** Luftwaffe temporarily switches to attacking British provincial cities, including Birmingham, Bristol, Coventry, Southampton, Liverpool, Plymouth

- **Nov 14/15** Luftwaffe inflicts massive destruction on central Coventry

ially attacks on London are ded to destroy the docks and and supply sources for the city. r realising that the Battle of n has been lost, the Luftwaffe to terrorise London and then cities to destroy British morale

- **Nov 16/17** Large RAF raid on Mannheim initiating city centres as targets instead of industry. This is in response to German raids on British cities and begins the strategy of 'area bombing'

- **Nov 16** Hamburg: first use of incendiaries to mark target

Sept 7 1940 to May 12 1941 Luftwaffe launches 71 major bombing raids on London, dropping over 18,000 tons of high-explosive. The 'Blitz' costs 43,000 British civilian lives, plus 139,000 injured. Luftwaffe losses are c.600 bombers

- **Dec 29** Devastating raid on London

Jan to March Luftwaffe gradually redeploys east to Bulgaria and Romania in readiness for the opening of the Eastern Front

Feb 10/11 ●
Stirling 4-engined heavy bombers make debut raid against oil tanks in Rotterdam

- **Feb 19 to May 12** Luftwaffe raids mainly against British ports

- **Feb 24/25** Manchester heavy bomber, precursor of the Lancaster, makes debut raid against Brest

January to April Luftwaffe intensifies bombing of Malta

March 31/April 1 ●
Emden: first RAF use of 4,000lb bomb

- **March 1** Bulgaria, under pressure, joins the Axis, leaving only Yugoslavia and Greece outside the Italo-German alliance

Jan 24 ●
Italians counter-attack in Albania

Jan 29 to March 29 British-US staff conference decides on 'Germany first' policy in the event of the USA joining hostilities

March 27 ●
Anti-Nazi coup d'état in Yugoslavia: Prince Paul ousted in favour of his heir, Prince Peter, with General Simovic as head of government

March 4 British troops begin redeployment to Greece

INVASION
ECE

8 Italians e Greece

Nov 4 Greeks unterattack d expel the lians from eece within ys, advancing o Albania until ted by bad ather

Nov 7 Roosevelt -elected as esident of the ited States for a cord third term

- **Nov 11/12** Taranto Raid. Aircraft from HMS *Illustrious* inflict serious damage on 3 Italian battleships in port. The Italian Fleet withdraws to the west of Italy

ov 5 British armed merchant cruiser s Bay, escorting convoy HX84, is sunk dmiral Scheer while the convoy scatters g just 5 of 37 merchantmen

NORTH AFRICA: The 'Compass' Offensive

- **Dec 9** British Western Desert Force, commanded by General O'Connor, opens offensive in North Africa after a 60-mile approach march

- **Dec 11** British take Sidi Barrani and nearby Italian positions

- **Jan 5** 6th Australian Div takes Bardia

- **Jan 7** British besiege Tobruk

Jan 22 ●
British capture Tobruk

Feb 6 ●
Australians take Benghazi

Feb 6–7 ●
Battle of Beda Fomm: 20,000 Italians surrender

- **Feb 12** Rommel arrives at Tripoli

- **Feb 14** Advance elements of German 5th Light Div arrive in Tripoli

March 24 ●
Rommel attacks El Agheila; British troops there withdraw

March 31 ●
Rommel attacks Agedabia and expels the British 2nd Armoured Div

NORTH AFRICA

EAST AFRICA: The Allied Reconquest

Jan 19 ●
British General Platt's forces invade Abyssinia from Sudan

Jan 20 ●
German Wannsee Conference: Heydrich co-ordinates plans for the Holocaust

- **Jan 31** 9th Indian Bde takes Metemma

- **Jan 24** From Kenya, General Cunningham invades southern Abyssinia and Italian Somaliland

25 Mogadishu taken

March 15–27 Final phase of battles for Keren

March 16 British forces cross from Aden to Berbera

March 28 ●
Battle of Cape Matapan. The British and Italian Fleets meet off Crete/Greece. The Italians are chased back to port with the loss of 3 cruisers and 2 destroyers

March 7/8 and 17 Three U-boat aces are lost – Prien (killed aboard U-47), Kretschmer (U-99) and Schepke (killed aboard U-99) – to British destroyers

Germans intervene in North Africa **11**

1941

APRIL	MAY	JUNE	JULY	AUGUS

● **July 8** Wilhelmshaven: **Aug 25,**
first RAF B-17 raid   Emden: las
B-17 ope

'THE BLITZ'

GERMAN INVASION OF RUSSIA

May 10/11 ●
Heaviest raid hits London, but
this is the last of the Blitz raids
and Luftwaffe units are moved
east preparatory to the invasion
of Russia

June 17 ●
Finland begins secretly to
mobilise. Allied with
Germany, Finland will
attack towards Leningrad

● **June 22** Germany
invades USSR

● **July 1**
Germans take
Riga

● **July 19** Hitler directs his
from the capture of Mosco
favour of thrusts against L
and Ukraine

● **July 2**
Germans
breach Stalin
Line into
Latvia

● **July 3**
290,000 Soviet
troops surrender
in the Bialystok
pocket, with
2,500 tanks

● **July 27**   Ge
Germans take   bes
Tallinin   Od

GERMAN CONQUEST
OF THE BALKANS

● **April 6** Germany invades
Yugoslavia and Greece

April 23 ●
Greece surrenders

● **April 13** Belgrade falls to the Germans

● **April 17** Yugoslavia capitulates

● **April 22–28** British troops
evacuate Greece

CRETE

May 20 ●   ● **May 28 to**
German   **June 1** British
airborne   evacuation of
invasion of   Crete
Crete begins

July 9 ●
Germans
take Vitebsk

● **July 15**
Germans create
Uman/Kiev/
Odessa and
Smolensk
encirclements

● **Aug 5 31**
Soviet troops
surrender in
Smolensk po

● **Aug 8 1**
Soviet troo
surrender i
Uman poc

June 29 ●
Finland attacks in the
Karelian Isthmus

● **July 12** Anglo-Soviet mutual
assistance pact signed

IRAQ

● **April 1**
Pro-German
Rashid Ali
seizes power

● **April 18** 10th
Indian Div begins
landing in the
Persian Gulf

● **May 9** British 'Habforce' brigade
enters Iraq

May 27 ●
Basra secured
by 10th
Indian Div

● **May 30** British
enter Baghdad,
Rashid Ali having
fled the previous day

● **July 15** Argentia,
Newfoundland, air base
established for US flights
to Britain

NORTH AFRICA

● **April 4** Rommel
takes Benghazi

● **April 7/8** Germans capture
British General O'Connor

● **April 11** Rommel
attacks Tobruk,
which holds out

● **April 11** Germans
advance to the
Egyptian frontier

NORTH AFRICA

● **May 15** British
'Brevity' offensive
into Libya repulsed

● **End May** Rommel reinforced
by 15th Panzer Division

● **June 15–17** British 'Battleaxe'
offensive in North Africa repulsed by
Rommel

● **July 5** Wavell replaced
by Auchinleck as Middle
East commander

Aug 19
Polish troo
over from Au
garrison of

● **May 10** Rudolf Hess
flies to Britain, where
he is imprisoned. Half a
century on, his mission
remains a mystery

● **July 4** Tito calls the
Yugoslavs to arms
against the Germans
and Italians

● **Aug 2** US-So
Lend-Lease beg
Iran will becom
important route
the supplies to
Russia

EAST AFRICA: The Allied Reconquest

● **April 6** Addis
Ababa captured

● **April 8** Capture
of Massawa
completes
the conquest
of Eritrea

● **April 2** 'Death ride of the
Italian Red Sea Squadron' –
sent on 'do or die' missions,
the 7 destroyers are sunk,
captured or run aground

● **May 5** Haile Selassie
enters Addis Ababa

May 27 ●
Fall of Gondar completes
elimination of the Italian
Empire in East Africa

SYRIA

● **June 8** British and Free
French invade Vichy Syria
and   ● **June 21** Free
Lebanon   French take Damascus

● **July 15**
Syria secured
by the Allies

Aug
Iran invaded by B
and Soviet f

Au
Cease-fire
British troo
meanwhile
the Abadan

May 8 Capture of German Enigma
code machine aboard U-110 by
HMS *Bulldog*; this helps British
codebreakers penetrate enemy
signals and locate U-boat groups

● **Aug**
Church
Roosev
confer
Placen
Newfo

THE BISMARCK SORTIE

● **May 18** North Atlantic sortie of German battleship
Bismarck and heavy cruiser *Prinz Eugen* begins

May 24 ●
British warships intercept
Bismarck and *Prinz Eugen* in the
Denmark Strait, and *Bismarck*
sinks the battlecruiser *Hood*

● **May 26** *Bismarck* damaged by
torpedo aircraft from carrier *Ark Royal*

● **May 27** *Bismarck* sunk; *Prinz
Eugen* meanwhile escapes to Brest

Sept 21 ●
First 'Arctic convoy' sails fro
Hvalfjord, Iceland, wit
munitions for Russia, arrivir
Archangel Aug 31 without lo:

12 *German invasion of the Balkans and Russia*

PTEMBER **OCTOBER** **NOVEMBER** **DECEMBER** **JANUARY**

29/30 Frankfurt: first raid
tralian squadrons in
r Command

● Nov 7/8 RAF large-scale raids
on Berlin, Mannheim and the
Ruhr suffer big losses

January
There are 262 air
raids on Malta

AN INVASION OF RUSSIA

pt 4
ans and
blockade
ngrad. The
will last
 900 days

● Sept 25 Germans
invade Crimea

● Oct 24 Germans
take Kharkov

● Nov 23 Germans are within 30 miles of Moscow

Dec 5 ● ● Dec 5–7 Soviet counterattacks from
Sudden freeze halts north and south of Moscow
German offensive 19
miles from Moscow

● Sept 30 Germans launch drive
on Moscow, Operation 'Typhoon'

ept 5 Hitler reverts
is original plan,
ing for Moscow

Oct 16 ● ● Oct 16 Muscovites
Germans   panic. Much of the
take   government moves
Odessa   beyond the Urals

● Dec 14–19 *German High Command
crisis:* Hitler takes personal command
ordering no further withdrawals

Sept 19 ●
mans take
Kiev and
600,000
oners plus
,500 tanks

Oct 27 ●
Germans secure most of
the Crimea

NORTH AFRICA
Nov 18 to Jan 6 British
'Crusader' offensive

Tobruk relieved Dec 7 ●

Jan 17 ● ● Jan 21
Bardia falls to Eighth Rommel
Army attacks

Jan 29 ●
Rommel takes Benghazi

Nov 24 ● ● Nov 25
Rommel makes abortive counter- British battleship
attack towards the Egyptian border *Barham* sunk in
Mediterranean

Jan 20 ●
Wannsee Conference. Heydrich
plans the 'Final Solution', the
extermination of the Jews

Sept 27 ●
US launches first
abricated Liberty
ship at Baltimore

Nov 13/14 ●
British carrier *Ark Royal*
sunk in Mediterranean

● Nov 18/19
Alexandria raid by
Italian frogmen cripples
two British battleships

Dec 22 to Jan 13 Allied 'Arcadia'
Conference, Washington

● Sept 18–28 First
transatlantic convoy
accompanied by
escort carrier,
Audacity

● Dec 17 First
Battle of Sirte
between Italians
and British

● Dec 11
Germany and
Italy declare
war on USA

Japanese invade Burma from central Thailand Jan 20 ●

Sept 26 ●
Vestern Desert
enamed Eighth
Army

● Dec 9
Japanese Fifteenth
Army enters Bangkok

● Dec 15 Japanese
enter Thailand in the
southern Kra Isthmus

● Jan 15 Japanese
advance up the Kra
Isthmus

MALAYA AND THE FALL OF SINGAPORE

Nov 26
Japanese strike force
leaves Hitokappu Bay in
the Kurile Islands,
beginning the 3,400-
mile voyage to Hawaii

Dec 8 ●
Japanese Twenty-fifth
Army lands in Malaya and
Thailand

Dec 25 ●
Hong Kong falls to the Japanese

Jan 11 ● ● Jan 15 Johore
Japanese enter Kuala defence line is
Lumpur   breached

Jan 31 ●
British withdraw to
Singapore Island

t 17 ●
ain and
occupy
an. The
dicates

Dec 7
Japanese naval aircraft
attack US Pacific Fleet
base at Pearl Harbor.
Almost all US aircraft
on the ground are
destroyed. US warships
sunk include 5
battleships and two
cruisers

PEARL HARBOR

PHILIPPINES: The Japanese Conquest

● Dec 8 Japanese
bombers destroy US Far
East Air Force

● Jan 9 Japanese
begin attacking the
Bataan defence line

Japanese invade Luzon Dec 10 ● ● Dec 22
Japanese land in Lingayen Gulf
and advance on Manila

● Jan 5 US withdrawal to
Bataan completed

● Jan 2 Japanese enter Manila

Jan 7 ●
Japanese secure Sarawak

● Jan 19
Japanese secure
North Borneo

Jan 11 ●
Japanese invade Borneo

Dec 9 ● ● Dec 10
Japanese take Tarawa and Makin Japanese take Guam

DUTCH EAST INDIES
● Jan 11 Japanese
invade Celebes

Dec 10 ●
British capital ships *Prince of Wales* and *Repulse* sunk
by land-based Japanese aircraft

● Jan 25
Japanese invade New Guinea

Pearl Harbor and War in the Far East **13**

1942

FEBRUARY	MARCH	APRIL	MAY	JUNE

February
There are 236 air raids on Malta

● **March 10/11** Essen: first Lancaster bombing mission

● **April 10/11** Essen: first RAF use of 8,000lb bomb

May 30/1 ●
Cologne: first '1,000-bomber' raid

RUSSIAN FRONT

● **Feb 8** 90,000 Germans encircled at Demyansk

March 19 ● Soviet Second Shock Army, part of the thrust to relieve Leningrad, cut off north of Novgorod

End March Soviet counterattacks stall, having failed to achieve significant success but having pushed the Germans back before Moscow

May 12 ● Soviets surprise the Germans near Kharkov

● **May 18** German offensive 'Fridericus' eliminates the salient gained by the Soviets at Isyum

June 22– Ger Kupy

● **Feb 4** Rommel halts west of Tobruk at the British Gazala Line

April to June Baedeker Raids: Luftwaffe attacks on British cities of Bath, Norwich, Exeter, Canterbury and York, all three-star cities in the famous tourist guidebook, in retaliation for RAF area bombing of Lübeck and Rostock

May 22 ● Germans encircle Kostenko's South-West Front

● **May 29** Germans eliminate the Kharkov pocket

Jun
G

● **May 8-16** Germans take Kerch

fron

Feb 11–13 The 'Channel Dash'. German raiders *Scharnhorst*, *Gneisenau* and *Prinz Eugen* return to German ports from Brest

● **March 6** German battleship *Tirpitz* sorties without success against Allied Arctic convoy PQ12, which is the last to reach Russia intact

By now U-boats deployed against US coastal shipping

April to June Germans drive against Tito's Yugoslav partisans in Bosnia farther west

t
Vo

● **April 16** Malta awarded George Cross by King George VI. From January to July there is only one 24-hour period without an air raid on the island

NORTH AFRICA

May 26 to June 13 Battle of Gazala

● **June 2-10** Ba the Cauldron

March 27/28 ●
British amphibious attack cripples strategically important dry dock at St-Nazaire

May 26–29 ● Rommel attacks the Gazala Line

June 11 ● Free French garrison at Bir Hacheim falls to Rommel

● **June** Battle Knight

● **March 22** 2nd Battle of Sirte Gulf

June 21 Romm tak Tobr

BURMA

British evacuate Rangoon

March 7 ●

● **March 13–20** British establish defensive line from Prome to Toungoo

● **March 29** The Chinese, almost encircled at Toungoo, escape north

May 11● Slim fights rearguard action at Kalewa

● **May 20** Burcorps enters India

BATTLE OF MIDWAY

March 12 ● Stilwell's Chinese Fifth and Sixth Armies hold the left flank against the Japanese

● **April 2** British retreat from Prome

● **Feb 5** Singapore surrenders

● **March 19** General Slim takes command of I Burma Corps (British and Indian troops in Burma)

● **April 12** Japanese take Myanaung

● **May 1** Japanese take Mandalay

May 27–28 Japanese forces leave Japan for Aleutians and Midway operations

● **June 2** US fo meet 350 miles of Midway

● **April 18** Doolittle raid on Tokyo

● **June 4** The exchange a se air attacks. Ja carriers *Soryu Kaga* sink. US *Yorktown* is cr

PHILIPPINES

MacArthur leaves the Philippines

March 11 ●

April 9 ● Allied forces in Bataan surrender

May 5 ● Japanese land on Corregidor

May 30 ● Nimitz sends his three carriers, with cruiser and destroyer support, to rendezvous off Midway

● **June 5** Two Japanese car are lost: *Aka* scuttled; *Hiry* after damage previous day

March 8 ● Japanese land at Salamau and Lae in New Guinea

May 7 ● Allied troops on Corregidor surrender

Feb 19 ● Battle of Lumbok Strait

● **Feb 27** Battle of the Java Sea

May 10 ● Surrender of the remaining Allied forces in the Philippines

● **June 6** Ja withdraw. U carrier *Yorkt* torpedoed a sinks next d

● **March 1** Battle of the Sunda Strait

BATTLE OF THE CORAL SEA

● **March 25** Japanese First Air Fleet enters the Indian Ocean and over two weeks attacks Colombo, raids British shipping, sinks two cruisers and carrier *Hermes*

● **May 1** US carriers rendezvous to halt Japanese invasion of Port Moresby

DUTCH EAST INDIES

Feb 14/15 ● Japanese landings on Sumatra

● **Feb 19** Japanese land on Timor

● **March 9** Dutch East Indies surrender

● **May 7–8** Battle of the Coral Sea. naval battle in which the opposing ships never sight each other directl Japanese Port Moresby invasion is postponed

14 *Japanese conquests to the turning-point at Midway*

JULY	AUGUST	SEPTEMBER	OCTOBER	NOVEMBER

Aug 11 ● thfinder Force established

● **Aug 17** Rouen: first European raid by US Eighth AF heavy bombers

N FRONT

30 German Sixth Army attacks st from the Kharkov area

3 Germans take Sevastopol

ly **5** Germans h Don River

July **7** Germans ke Voronezh

' to July **11** f Arctic PQ17. of 34 t through

● **Aug 5** Germans take Voroshilovsk

● **Aug 19** The Battle of Stalingrad begins as Paulus attacks the city

● **Sept 6** Germans take Novorossisk

● **Aug 15** Germans reach the foothills of the Caucasus mountains

● **Aug 19 to end Sept** Soviet attempts to relieve Leningrad fail

Aug 10–15 Gibraltar-Malta convoy 'Pedestal' saves Maltese from starvation. On 11th aircraft carrier *Eagle* is sunk

● **Sept 20** Paulus calls for reinforcements. Soviet defenders are now penned into 10x4-mile area along the west bank of the Volga

● **Sept 28** Germans renew the battle for Stalingrad, but the struggle for the city has reached stalemate

● **Nov 19** Soviet offensive to cut off Stalingrad begins

Nov 23 ● Soviet pincers close, trapping German Sixth and part of Fourth Panzer Army

Nov 24 ● Luftwaffe plans to resupply Paulus's trapped forces by air: but capacity falls far short of need

● **Nov 11** Germans occupy Vichy France

AFRICA

27 1st f El . Rommel sed

June **26–29** Germans take Mersa Matruh

gomery takes command of the ghth Army. Alexander becomes verall commander Middle East

● **Aug 3** Churchill visits Cairo and reorganises the local command

Aug 18 ●

● **Aug 19** Canadian and British amphibious raid on Dieppe fails disastrously

Aug 30 to Sept 2 Battle of Alam Halfa. Rommel is again repulsed. Both sides begin to reinforce and regroup

Sept 13/14 ● British land and sea raids on Tobruk, Benghazi and Barce fail

Oct 23 to Nov 4 Battle of El Alamein

Nov 6–7 ● British pursue retreating Germans hampered by heavy rain

Nov 8 ● 'Torch' Landings in Morocco and Algeria meet Vichy French resistance

Germans deploy to Tunisia **Nov 9** ●

Nov 15–16 ● Allied forces advance slowly into Tunisia, hampered by rain

● **Nov 13** British retake Tobruk

● **Nov 11** Armistice in Morocco and Algeria

PUA-NEW GUINEA: BUNA-GONA AND THE KOKODA TRAIL

July **7** Allied Maroubra rce ascends the arduous koda Trail at the centre the Owen anley Mts

July **23** ● anese eject oubra Force om Kokoda

nese forced to evacuate Milne Bay **Sept 4–6** ●

● **Aug 18-21** Japanese land in force at Buna

Aug 25–29 ● Japanese land in Milne Bay; the Allies deploy forces to meet them

Mid-Aug Australian troops arrive at Port Moresby

● **Aug 29** Japanese push Australians on the Kokoda Trail back to Myola

● **Aug 21** Australians meet Maroubra Force

● **Sept 24** Japanese pull back on the Kokoda Trail

● **Sept 15** US reinforcements arrive at Port Moresby

● **Oct 6** US force advances along the Kapa Kapa Track to outflank Kokoda; other forces land at Pongani, south of Buna

● **Nov 2** Allies take Kokoda

Nov 16 ● Allies begin attacking Gona

Nov 18–19 ● Allies arrive before Buna-Gona

GUADALCANAL

une / July ese on canal egin g an eld

Aug 9 ● Battle for Savo Island

Aug 7 ● US landings on Guadalcanal and surrounding islands

● **Aug 8** US troops seize Japanese airfield and name it Henderson Field

● **Aug 24** Battle of the Eastern Solomons

Aug 30 US occupies Adak in the Aleutians

● **Sept 12–14** Battle of 'Bloody Ridge'. Japanese fail to retake Henderson Field

Sept 10 to Nov 5 British take control of Madagascar

● **Oct 23–26** Battle for Henderson Field. Major Japanese air/land/sea offensive defeated

Oct 26 ● Battle of Santa Cruz Islands

● **Oct 11** Battle of Cape Esperance

● **Nov 1–4** US forces take the offensive

Nov 12–13 ● First Naval Battle of Guadalcanal

Nov 14–15 ● Second Naval Battle for Guadalcanal is the last major attempt by the Japanese to land reinforcements

---

Turning the tide: Stalingrad, El Alamein and Guadalcanal **15**

1942/1943

| DECEMBER | JANUARY | FEBRUARY | MARCH | APRIL |

Jan 12–18 Soviet offensive lifts the blockade of Leningrad

● **Jan 30/31** Hamburg: first use of H2S

● **March 5/6** Essen: first raid in Battle of the Ruhr

● **April 1** Plan, Con Bomber O

EASTERN FRONT: STALINGRAD

Dec 12 ● German counter-attack to relieve Paulus

The Soviets aim at the flanks of von Manstein's line, held by Italians in the north and Romanians in the south

Jan 3 ● Germans begin evacuation of the Caucasus area south of the Manych River

● **Dec 28** The German relief attempt has failed. Hitler agrees to a withdrawal, which will leave Stalingrad 125 miles behind the Soviet lines

● **Jan 10** Soviet offensive to destroy German Sixth Army cut off in Stalingrad

Jan 13-18 Soviet offensives across the Don River

Jan 31 to Feb 2 Germans at Stalingrad surrender

● **Feb 8** Soviets take Kursk

Feb 16 ● Germans evacuate Kharkov

● **Feb 20** Von Manstein's offensive surprises the Soviet Voronezh and South-West Fronts

April 13 ● Germans announce discovery of the grave marking the Katyn massacre of Polish officers, perpetrated by the Soviets in spring 1940 near Smolensk

● **March 4–15** The second phase of Manstein's offensive retakes Kharkov

Von Manstein has now eliminated the Soviet salient south of Kursk; the spring thaw and resulting mud postpones further operations against the Kursk salient

A to W G u b

NORTH AFRICA

Nov 27 to Dec 28 Allied forces meet stiff resistance in northern Tunisia

Dec 24 ● Admiral Darlan assassinated

● **Dec 17** British 14th Division advances down Burma coast toward Akyab, beginning First Arakan Campaign

Jan 23 ● Rommel enters Tunisia and fortifies the Mareth Line

Jan 18 ● Axis offensive in central Tunisia secures Eastern Dorsals passes

● **Jan 30–31** Allied Casablanca Conference

● **Feb 1–3** British attacks repulsed north of Akyab

Feb 14–22 Von Arnim and Rommel attack across Eastern Dorsals to Kasserine Pass

March 6 ● Battle of Medenine: Rommel's pre-emptive strike against Eighth Army repulsed

● **Feb 28** Vermork raid: commandos cripple German atomic research plant in Norway

● **March 7** Japanese attack on the east bank of the Mayu River

Feb 26 to March 19 Allied offensive in the north fails to break through

March 17–31 Patton's II Corps th in the southern Eastern Dorsals ta Gafsa and Maknassy pass

March 20–28 Eighth Arm breaks through the Maret

March–Ma Climax of the B the Atlantic

● **April 3** Jap cut off and ca British brigade Indin

PAPUA-NEW GUINEA

Dec 2–14 Japanese reinforcements arrive in Buna-Gona area

Jan 2 ● Allies take Buna Mission

The Kokoda/Buna-Gona campaign is fought during bad weather in mountainous terrain, imposing a terrible strain on the soldiers of both sides

Early Jan Japanese reinforce Lae and Salamaua and advance inland

● **Jan 12** US land on Amchitka and build an airfield to attack Kiska

BURMA: First Chindit Expedition

Feb 13/14 ● Wingate's Chindits cross Chindwin into Burma to cut Myitkyina–Mandalay railway

● **March 3–4** Chindits clash with Japanese, now aware of their presence

Of 3,000 Chindits on the first expedition, nearly a third will not get back to India

● **March 6** Chindits destroy railway then Wingate crosses Irrawaddy Rive destroy the Gokteik Gorge viaduct, will cut the Lashio–Mandalay Road

● **March 8** Japanese offensive up Yangtse River, essentially a large-scale raid

● **March 28** Win attempt to cross t Irrawaddy at Inyw repulsed. Chindits up into small part exfiltrate during A

● **March 11** US Fourteenth Air F established in China under Chen

GUADALCANAL

Nov 30 Battle of Tassafaronga

● **Dec 9** 1st Marine Division relieved by XIV Corps

Dec 15 to Jan 26 US drives Japanese from Mount Austen area

December Stilwell begins building the Ledo Road, Assam to China via north Burma

Jan 22–23 ● The westward push continues: Japanese cleared from Kokumbona

● **Jan 31** The Battle of the Barents Sea

Feb 9 ● Americans finally secure Guadalcanal

● **Feb 1–8** Japanese withdraw from Doma Cove onboard destroyers

Feb 28 ● Ledo Road reaches Burma frontier from China, but construction is then delayed by rain

● **March 3–5** Battle of the Bismarck Sea

April 18 ● Japanese CinC Combined Fleet Admiral Yamamoto killed over Bougainville, after 'Magic' intelligence forewarns fleet of his itinerary

● **March 26** Battle of the Komandorski Islands (Bering Sea

1943

| MAY | JUNE | JULY | AUGUST | SEPTEMBER |

/17 ● usters' raid

● **July 9/10** Gelsenkirchen: last raid in Battle of the Ruhr

● **July 24 to Aug 3** Hamburg raids cause firestorm

● **Aug 17/18** Germans' Peenemünde V-weapon research site bombed by RAF

N FRONT

Kursk salient: Germans plan major encirclement; Soviets build three lines of defence and deploy a force to counter-strike once Germans are repulsed

July 5–13 Battle of Kursk

Russian Autumn Offensive ● **Aug 23** Soviets retake Kharkov

● **July 17** Russians thrust towards Kharkov

July 5 ● German Ninth Army attacks from north; Fourth Panzer Army and Group Kempff attack from south. These two pincers are aimed at Kursk

● **July 12** Soviets counterattack the southern pincer at Prokhorovka in the largest tank battle of World War II and halt the German advance

● **Aug 5** Soviets take Orel and Belgorod while Germans fall back to Hagen Line before Bryansk

● **Aug 26** Soviets strike Army Group Centre in the south

● **Sept 14** Soviet Central and Voronezh Fronts attack toward Kiev

May-June partisans are trapped by Germans in Montenegrin ntains, but escape with heavy loss

July 15 ● Soviets counterattack the northern pincer

● **July 16** Germans fall back

● **Aug 30** Soviets take Taganrog, threatening Germans in the Taman peninsula

● **Sept 25** Soviets take Roslavl and Smolensk

Kursk is the last major German offensive on the Russian front. For the Soviets it marks the beginning of a series of massive offensives that will take them to Berlin and Vienna

● **Aug 12** Hitler orders construction of the East Wall defence line

ay 7 Allies Tunis and rta

● **May 29 to June 3** Allied Algiers Conference

ALLIED LIBERATION OF SICILY

ITALY: Allied Landings

● **Sept 3** British XIII Corps crosses to the toe of Italy

● **May 11** Allies finally secure Tunisia

July 10 ● Allies invade Sicily. Patton's Seventh Army lands on south coast; Montgomery's Eighth Army to south-east

● **July 13/14–16** Battle for the Primasole Bridge

● **Aug 3** Axis forces begin evacuation across the Strait of Messina

● **July 23** Patton's forces take Palermo then swing east for Messina

Sept 9 Allied landings at Salerno by Clark's US Fifth Army and at Taranto by Montgomery's Eighth Army

Sept 9–17 Battle of Salerno

y 4 nese

cling gdaw

4 ● nese take gdaw ritish draw

● **May 24** Disastrous U-boat losses in May – 41 boats – cause Dönitz temporarily to withdraw his boats from the North Atlantic

July 10 ● Syracuse taken

July 16 ● Patton advances rapidly towards Palermo

Aug 5 ● Montgomery takes Catania

Aug 17 Patton's troops enter Messina. But the Axis have evacuated successfully

● **Sept 3** Italy signs armistice with the Allies effective 8th

Hitler sends Rommel with German troops into northern Italy following the fall of Mussolini

July 25 ●

● **Sept 12** Daring German rescue of Mussolini from Gran Sasso in the mountains north-east of Rome by Skorzeny's special forces

July 4 ● Death of Sikorsky, leader of the Free Poles, in an air crash

Aug 13–23 Allied 'Quadrant' Conference, Quebec

ay 12–15 Allied ident' Conference, ashington

NEW GEORGIA

● **Sept 11** Japanese evacuate Salamaua to Lae

TIANS s n u

June 21 ● US invades New Georgia

July 17/18 ● Japanese counter-attack

● **July 25** Reinforced, US forces begin major attack

● **Aug 25** US secures New Georgia

July 3–4 ● US makes new landings on New Georgia

Aug 5 ● US take Munda

● **Aug 13** US activates Munda airfield

● **Sept 12** Australians take Lae and its airfield

June 29 ● MacArthur launches the 'Cartwheel' offensive against Rabaul, the main Japanese base in the area. This involves the clearance of the Solomons including Bougainville, and New Georgia

July 28/29 Under cover of fog, Japanese complete evacuation of Kiska

Sept 4 ● Australian 9th Division lands near Lae in New Guinea

● **Sept 16** Australians take Salamaua

● **May 30** US secure Attu after a hard fight in foul weather. Most surviving Japanese commit suicide

● **July 5/6** Naval clash in the Gulf of Kula off New Georgia

Aug 1943 The Allies deem Rabaul effectively neutralised, isolated by advances on New Guinea and neighbouring islands

September Reconstruction of the Burma Road begins

● **July 12/13** Battle of Kolombangara

● **Aug 6/7** Battle of the Vella Gulf

Kursk, Sicily and Italy: the Allies invade mainland Europe **17**

1943/1944

● Nov 18/19 ●
Aerial Battle of Berlin begins

● Dec 13 Long-range P-51B
Mustang fighters fly first
escort mission to Kiel.

● Feb 20/21 'Big Week'
bombing offensive on Ge
fighter and ball-bearing f

EASTERN FRONT

● Oct 6 Soviets
attack between
German Army
Groups North
and Centre
toward Vitebsk

– Sept 26 Soviets
bridge the
Dnieper River

– End Sept
Von Manstein
has withdrawn
behind the
East Wall

Autumn 1943
German Army Group North
constructs the Panther
defence line as a fallback

● Nov 12 ●
Soviets take
Zhitomir,
effectively
breaching the
German East
Wall

● Nov 3
Soviets
attack from the
Dnieper bridgehead
at Lyutezh

● Nov 6
Soviets
take Kiev

● Nov 16 Germans
secure Dodecanese

Oct
Soviets
attack
toward the

● Nov 18
Germans
retake
Zhitomir

Nov 26 ●
Soviets
take
Gomel

To Dec
Generally from
north of Vitebsk
to the Baltic the
front lines are
relatively stable

Oct to Jan
Further German
offensives
against Tito's
Yugoslavs

Nov 28 to Dec 6
Allied 'Eureka'
Conference, Tehran

● Dec 24 Soviets
attack from the Kursk
salient

● Jan 8
Soviets take
Kirovograd

Jan 14–15 ●
Soviets launch
offensive to clear
Leningrad area

Jan 27 ● ● Jan 30
Soviets attack west Soviets attack in
from Korosten the Dnieper bend

January
Eisenhower and Montgomery
depart Italian theatre to
prepare for the invasion of
North-West Europe

● Jan 26
Soviets end
Leningrad
blockade

● Jan 25–
28 Soviets
encircle two
German corps
west of
Cherkassy

Lenir
offensive
Finland
tries to
negotiat
US

Feb 2
Sovi
t
Kri
F

By the enc
February ov
million US t
have been trar
across the A

ITALY

● Oct 1 Foggia captured
by Eighth Army, Naples by
Fifth Army

● Oct 3–6 Battle of Termoli

Oct 12–15
Crossing of the
Volturno Line

● Oct 3
Germans take
Cos in the
Dodecanese

● Oct 2 On New Guinea:
Australians take Finschhafen,
but stiff resistance persists
inland

● Dec 8 Sattelberg Mountain, Japanese
focus of resistance west of Finschhafen, is
taken. After mopping-up, the Australians
pursue the Japanese north

October: Burma
Stilwell's Chinese
advance in N Burma,
building Ledo Road.
Completion of Japanese
Burma–Thailand railway

October: Borneo
Chinese population of
British Borneo stage an
uprising against
Japanese, but are
defeated

● Oct 6 Battle
of Vella Lavella

Nov 1/2 ●
Battle of Empress
Augusta Bay

● Nov 8 Eighth
Army reaches
Sangro River

Nov 20 ●
Eighth
Army
crosses
Sangro

Nov 5–15 First
Battle for Camino

Nov 23–26
Allied 'Sextant'
Conference, Cairo

● Nov 1 Large-scale
US invasion of
Bougainville, which is
heavily garrisoned by
the Japanese

● Nov 7–8 Japanese counterattack
US Marines on Bougainville

GILBERT ISLANDS

Nov 20 ●
US come ashore on
Tarawa and Makin

● Nov 23 Tarawa and
Makin secured by US after
Japanese fight to the death

● Nov 24/25 Battle
of Cape St George

● Nov 28
Eighth Army
attacks Gustav
Line

Nov 29 to
Dec 1 Battle of
Sangro River

Dec 20–28 1st
Canadian Div
takes Ortona

Jan 17
Fifth Army attacks
across the Garigliano
River but is halted
before Monte Cassino

Dec 2–10 Second Battle for Monte
Camino: Fifth Army resumes
attacks toward the Gustav Line

● Dec 4–7 First Battle of Orsonga;
subsequent battles 18th and 23rd

Dec 26 ●
Battle of the North Cape: British sink
German battlecruiser *Scharnhorst*

Operation 'Hailstone': massive air raids on Truk from 9
US carriers destroy 265 aircraft and 140,000 tons of
shipping, effectively neutralising the Japanese base

● Dec 4 Kwajalein
and Wotje in the
Marshall Islands
bombed by US
carrier aircraft

● Jan 22 Anzio landings b
VI Corps establishes beach
which fails to be exploited

● Feb 3 and
Feb 16–19 Ge
counterattack
destroy the A
beachhead

Jan 24 to Feb 11
First Battle of
Monte Cassino

Feb 15 ●
Allies destroy monastery of
Monte Cassino from the air

Feb 17–18 ●

Fe
Secon
of Mc
Cassin

Feb 3 ●
Japanese offensive in the
Arakan area, outflanking the
Allied line inland to Taung
Bazaar, intending to encircle
the defenders

● Jan 2 US landing
at Saidor on New
Guinea just fails to
cut off the Japanese
retreat north from
the Huon Peninsula

● Dec 26 US main
landings on New Britain
at Cape Gloucester

● Feb 5 Ch
enter Burm
Ledo

F
US lar
Admiralty Isl
establish ai

MARSHALL ISLA

● Feb 1–4 US I
on and capture
Kwajalein

Feb 18–23
Eniwetok invad
and captu

1944

MARCH	APRIL	MAY	JUNE	JULY

● **March 24/25** Last major RAF raid of the aerial Battle of Berlin

June 13 ●
German V-1 flying-bombs launched against London

July 27 ●
Homberg: first major RAF daylight raid

[EASTE]RN FRONT

[Marc]h 1 Soviets [tak]e Panther [...] the Estonian [...]o which [...]nth Army has [...]wn

● **March 28** German First Panzer Army encircled east of Podgaitsy

March 30 to April 7 German First Panzer Army breaks out

I March 30 Hitler sacks Manstein and von Kleist

June 9 ●
Soviet summer offensive Operation 'Bagration' begins in the north

May 25 ●
German special forces fail in attempt to seize Tito at Drvar

June 27 ●
Soviets take Vitebsk

July 4 ●
Soviets take Minsk

June 22 ●
Operation 'Bagration' begins in the center

July 20 ● Soviets reach the Polish border

July 20 ●
Attempt on Hitler's life at Rastenburg (bomb plot) fails

● **July 23** Soviets take Lublin

[Mar]ch 4–6 [...] offensive [...] of the Pripet [...] and across [...]ug River

● **April 10** Soviets take Odessa

May 5–12 Soviets assault Sevastopol and secure Crimea

FINLAND

June 10 ●
Soviets attack on the Finnish front

June 20 ●
Soviets take Vipurii

July 26 ●
Soviets reach the Vistula River

● **March 17** Soviet Second Ukrainian Front reaches the Dniester River

[...]3 ● [...]take [...]rson

● **April 2** Soviets enter Romania

NORTH-WEST EUROPE: D-Day

June 6 ●
D-Day: Allies land 155,000 troops in Normandy

● **June 11–14** British 7th Amd Div thrust halted at Villers-Bocage

● **July 17** Rommel wounded

■ *Stalemate in Italy*

April 29–30 Final air strike by US carrier aircraft on Truk wrecks what ships and installations remain. The Japanese base is destroyed

June 19–22 ●
Storms in the Channel damage Mulberry harbours

● **June 26–30** British fail to break out west of Caen

[...] to March 3 [...]ued German [...] on the Anzio [...]ead

June 7–8, 11–14 Canadians and British forces fail to take Caen

July 18 ●
British and Canadians secure Caen but are halted at Bourgebus Ridge

[...] 15–25 [...] Battle of [...]e Cassino

● **April 17** Japanese Ichi-Go offensive in southern China. The Japanese overrun Fourteenth Air Force airfields

ITALY

May 11/12 to June 4 Allied offensive to breach Gustav Line and take Rome

● **June 22–27 July 25–27** Allies take Cherbourg US forces break out of beachhead

● **March 24** Wingate killed in an air crash

May 18 ●
Monte Cassino finally falls to the Poles

● **May 23** Allies break out of Anzio beachhead

July 18 ●
Allies take Ancona

[M]arch 5–12 Second [Chin]dit mission cuts [Man]dalay to Myitkyina [...]ay

May 17 ●
Chindits handed to Stilwell's command

● **June 4** US Fifth Army enters Rome

July 19 ●
Allies take Livorno

● **March 24** Chindits fail in attempt to take Indaw but repulse more Japanese attacks on their fortified areas

PAPUA-NEW GUINEA: Hollandia

● **April 22** US landings at Hollandia and Aitape

June 6–27 Chindits capture Mogaung

● **July 9** Saipan secured. 243 Japanese troops, women and children throw themselves off Marpi Point cliffs

[...]March 7/8 [Jap]anese begin [the]ir invasion of [Ind]ia

April 5–18 Japanese besiege Kohima, which is resupplied by air

● **May 27** US land on Biak Island and secure it on June 30

● **May 11** 1944 Chinese offensive begins from Yunnan across the Salween River

MARIANAS

June 15–17 US landings on Saipan, with heavy casualties

July 6/7 ●
Japanese final suicide counterattack

July 21 ●
US land on Guam

● **March 11** British retake Buthidaung, east of Maungdaw, then redeploy two divisions north to the Imphal-Kohima area

● **April 18** British relieve Kohima

● **April 22** British begin pushing the Japanese back from Kohima. The Imphal-Kohima area is cleared of Japanese by June 22

BATTLE OF THE PHILIPPINE SEA

June 13 ●
Japanese Admiral Ozawa is tasked with stopping the invasion of Saipan and destroying the US carriers. He has 9 carriers, US Fifth Fleet has 15

● **June 19** Japanese 373-plane attack on US carriers; 243 Japanese aircraft are downed for the loss of 29 Americans and US submarines sink 2 carriers

[Ja]panese attack Imphal from the [...]east but are halted at Sengmai

April 18 Japanese attack Imphal from the east

May 17 ●
Merrill's Marauders take Myitkyina airfield but cannot take the town

● **June 20** US sink another carrier, but 80 aircraft are lost during the return, running out of fuel or crash-landing

[Mar]ch 24 Final [Japa]nese attack on [U]S Bougainville [b]eachhead fails

Imphal-Kohima is the turning-point in Burma

This is the largest carrier battle of the war, 'the Great Marianas Turkey-Shoot', leaving Ozawa just 35 aircraft

D-Day, Imphal-Kohima and Rome 19

Sept 8 ●
German V-2 rocket offensive against London begins

Sept 17 to Oct 3 Lull in German V-2 attacks on London as Allies capture forward launch sites

Oct 1944
Belgian cities attacked by V-1s

EASTERN FRONT

● **Aug 1** Polish uprising in Warsaw fails to get Soviet support. Despite aid parachuted from the West, the Germans suppress the rising by Oct 2

● **Aug 30** Soviets secure Ploesti oilfields in Romania

● **Aug 31** Soviets enter Bucharest

● **Sept 8** Bulgaria declares war on Germany

● **Sept 14** Soviet offensive in Estonia and Latvia

Oct 5–10 Soviets advance in Lithuania to the Baltic coast, trapping German forces in the Courland Peninsula

● **Sept 28** Soviets attack toward Belgrade in conjunction with Tito's partisans from the south-west

● **Oct 15** Soviets take Riga

Oct 29 to Dec 5 Soviets attack and encircle Budapest

Oct 7–15 Soviets take Petsamo, northern Finland

Nov 23 ●
Soviets take Cop, strategic rail junction in Hungary

Nov 21 ●
Albanian partisans take Tirana and Durazzo

Dec 9 ●
Soviets reach Danube N of Vac

● **Dec 4** Soviet advance on a front in Hung Lake Balaton

● **Nov 29** German evacuate Scutari

● **Nov 29** Soviets northern Finland

● **De** Sovie Czech slova

Aug 25 ●
The Finns ask Soviets for peace terms and an armistice is signed on Sept 19

NORTH-WEST EUROPE: Breakout

● **Aug 7/8** Canadian offensive toward Falaise

Aug 21 ●
Falaise pocket closed. 50,000 Germans surrender

● **Sept 3** British take Brussels

● **Aug 25** French and US troops enter Paris

Sept 12–14 Allied 'Octagon' Conference, Quebec

Sept 17–26 Battle of Arnhem: Allied airborne attack fails to penetrate German line ●

Oct 21 US take Aachen

Oct 1 to Nov 8 Canadians clear the Scheldt estuary

● **Oct 4** British land at Patra in Greece

Nov 1–8 British and Canadian amphibious attack secures Walcheren

● **Nov 16** US launch thrust for Cologne

● **Nov 7** Roosevelt re-elected President of the USA for unique 4th term

Nov 12 ●
British air attack on *Tirpitz* succeeds, eliminating German threat to Arctic convoys

BATTLE O BULGE

Dec 16 to German A offensive of the Bul

● **De** Sie Ba

● **Dec 3** Civil breaks out in A

● **Dec 4** Can enter Ravenn

● **Aug 31** British take Amiens

● **Aug 15** Allied landings in Provence

● **Aug 19** Paris uprising

Aug 30 to Sept 2 Battle for the Gothic Line

Sept 22 to Dec 29 Battles of the Italian Rivers: Uso, Fiumicino, Savio, Ronco and Lamonte

ITALY

● **Aug 4** Allies reach Arno Line and take Florence

Sept 2 ● Allies take Pisa

Sept 4–9 and 12–21 Battles of Coriano

● **Sept 21** Greek Bde of Eighth Army takes Rimini

August Last Chindit elements flown out from Burma to India

● **Sept 26** Japanese armies in Burma move to an essentially defensive posture. General Kimura intends to hold a line from Akyab via Mandalay to Lashio

Nov 19
In Burma, Slim begins a general offensive on a 140-mile front, initially, crossing the Chindwin at Sittaung

● **Dec 3** In Bu Fourteenth Ar crosses the Ch at Kalewa and Mawlaik, linki with Sultan's fl flank. Japanes resistance (Fif Army)

● **Aug 3** Stilwell's Chinese take Myitkyina

Late Aug Japanese push Chinese back to the Salween River

Sept 15 ● US forces land on Morotai and on Peleliu in the Palaus

PHILIPPINES

● **Oct 20** US main landings in Leyte Gulf by Kreuger's Sixth Army after 4hr barrage. A fleet of more than 700 ships lands 160,000 men. This day MacArthur also makes his personal return to the Philippines

Dec 7 ● US forces land at Ormoc, on the western coast of Leyte Island

Mid–August Burma Road reconstruction completed

Oct 25
First large scale deployment of Kamikaze against the US escort carriers at Leyte Gulf

● **D** US land unop on t coas Min

MARIANAS

● **Aug 10** US secure Guam

July 30 US land at the NW tip of New Guinea

Oct 20–22
Admiral Ozawa sails with carriers towards the Philippines to lure US carriers away while, from Brunei Bay, Kurita's fleet sails to hit US invasion fleet at Leyte

Oct 25
Battle of Surigao Strait: US sink 5 of the 7 Japanese ships including battleships *Fuso* and *Yamashiro*

BATTLE OF LEYTE GULF

● **Oct 24** Battle of the Sibuyan Sea; giant battleship *Musashi* sunk

● **Oct 24/25** Halsey turns north to find Ozawa Kurita reverses course to pass through San Bern Strait and hit the US Leyte invasion fleet from th

● **Oct 25** Battle off Samar: Kurita's force surpr escort carriers of Admiral Sprague

Oct 25 Battle of Cape Engaño: Halsey locate Ozawa's fleet and sinks the carriers before t south too late to trap Kurita

Dec US forces s Leyte

Leyte Gulf is the largest naval engagement of all time

1945

Germans'
·latte' air
·e in the west

● **Feb 13/14** Dresden bombed by RAF and USAAF. Firestorm kills c.50,000

● **April 29** Operation 'Manna' aerial food supply to Netherlands begins

RN FRONT: GERMANY AND BERLIN

·an 20 ●
·s troops
·Germany
·Namslau

● **End Jan** There are now over 50 German divisions cut off in Courland and in East Prussia

March 1 Zhukov's Front strikes north into Pomerania

April 16 ● Zhukov and Konev begin Soviet drive to Berlin

BATTLE FOR BERLIN

May 2 ●
Berlin surrenders to the Soviets

● **May 10** German Army Group Centre surrenders to Soviets

● **Jan 14–17** Soviets encircle and capture Warsaw

● **Feb 8** Konev's Front attacks toward the Neisse River, encircling Breslau and Glogau

March 25 ●
Soviets reach Gulf of Danzig

April 17 Zhukov's Front takes the Seelow Heights

● **May 14** German Army Group East surrenders to Tito's forces

·ts take Budapest **Feb 13** ●

March 5/6 ●

March 30 ●
Soviets take Danzig

April 18 ●
Zhukov crosses the Spree River

● **April 25** Soviets encircle Berlin

·German 'Spring Awakening' offensive opens in southern Hungary but soon loses momentum

● **April 13** Soviets take Vienna

·-WEST EUROPE

RHINELAND AND GERMANY

·16 ●
·pinch
·r' the
·ulge'

Jan 20 to Feb 5 French and US forces encircle 8 German divisions in the Colmar pocket

● **April 1** US forces complete encirclement of the Ruhr, trapping Army Group B. 325,000 Germans surrender on 18th

● **April 30** Hitler commits suicide

● **Jan 23** Allies take St-Vith

● **Feb 8 to March 10** Allied 'Veritable', 'Grenade' and 'Blockbuster' offensives from the Roer to the Rhine

Rhine bridge captures:
March 7 US First Army at Remagen, **March 22–27** US at Boppard, St Goar and at Worms, **March 23/24** British and Canadians north of the Lippe, **March 22/23** US Third Army at Oppenheim, **March 31** French near Germersheim

● **May 4** Montgomery receives German surrender in NW Germany, Netherlands and Denmark at Lüneburg Heath

·31/Jan 1 Germans 'Nordwind' offensive ·sace

April 25 ●
US and Soviet forces meet at Torgau on the Elbe River

● **May 7** Germans surrender to Eisenhower at Reims

● **Jan 30** ·r 6,000 refugees as German liner ·n Gustlov, out of ·zig, is torpedoed

Feb 4–11 Allied Yalta Conference

April 19 ●
US take Leipzig

May 8 ●
Berlin surrender ceremony to Soviet, US, British and French representatives. This day becomes VE Day

·e Peace of Varkiza proves ·e temporary, civil war ·h returning to Greece in ·e 1946–49 ·s

Feb 12 In the final months of hostilities between 1,500,000 and 2,000,000 refugees are evacuated by sea from Germany's eastern provinces in the path of the Soviet advance

● **April 12** US President Roosevelt dies. Vice-President Harry H. Truman succeeds him

·AA

ITALY: Final Offensive

·se from Yunnan ·eet at Mongyu, ·ing the Ledo to ·rma Road and ·ng India-China ·ommunications

● **Jan 27**

March 7 ● Opening of final Allied Chinese take Lashio offensive in Italy

April 9 **April 21** ● Poles take Bologna

● **April 25** Allies take Verona and Parma

● **April 29** German forces in Italy surrender, effective May 2

● **Feb 15–21** US take the Bataan peninsula

● **March 20** British secure Mandalay

● **April 28** Mussolini executed by communist partisans who ambush his convoy

·HILIPPINES

Jan 9 US landing at ·ngayen Gulf, Luzon

Feb 26 ●
Corregidor secured. The Japanese detonate the magazine there

● **March 3** Manila secured, but most of the city is in ruins

April 1 ●
US forces land on the west coast of Okinawa

OKINAWA
April 16–21
US invade and clear Ie Shima island

● **May 3** Rangoon secured

·8 US reach ·—
·outskirts of
·a, which is
·by 25,000
·ese troops.
·nd-to-hand
·an fighting
·in some of
·the worst
·ction in the
·Pacific War

IWO JIMA

Feb 19 ●
US Marines go ashore on Iwo Jima

Feb 21 ●
Some 50 Kamikaze suicide bombers from Tokyo strike the US invasion fleet

Iwo Jima is America's most costly battle of World War II

● **Feb 23** US take Mount Suribachi, a 500-foot high extinct volcano

March 24
US land on Kerama Islands SW of Okinawa

March 25
Iwo Jima secure

April 6–7 ●
Kamikaze attacks on US invasion fleet hits 28 ships and sinks 3

March 26 ●
Japanese mount final, suicidal banzai charge on Iwo Jima. Of the 22,000-man garrison, only 216 survive as PoWs

April 9 US forces attack the formidable defence lines based on Shuri castle

● **April 20** US clear north of Okinawa

May 27–29 ●
US take Shuri castle

● **April 6** Battleship *Yamato* sails from Japan's Inland Sea on a suicide mission to intervene in the Okinawa landing and is sunk next day off Kyushu

1945

JUNE	JULY	AUGUST	SEPTEMBER	OCTOBE

US bombers hit 60 smaller cities and towns in Japan with incendiaries and high-level precision bombing. The Japanese oil industry is destroyed

June: There are so few Japanese fighters left that they are grounded to preserve them for use in the expected Allied invasion of Japan. **By end July** US bombers have practically run out of targets. Civilian casualties are over 800,000 including 300,000 dead. Some eight and a half million people are homeless

By June MacArthur has control of Luzon and most cities and towns in the Philippines have been secured. Japanese resistance continues in isolated groups in the mountains

BURMA

July 19 ● Japanese attack near Taungoo to re-establish contact with forces trapped on western side of the Sittang, after a feint farther south toward Waw on 3rd–11th

After the Japanese Taungoo offensive, there are no further major military operations, mopping up continuing until the surrender

● **June 6** Japanese government resolves to fight to the end

● **June 22** Japanese Emperor Hirohito tells his government that peace must be sought

● **July 1** Australians land in Brunei

● **June 10** Australians take Balikpapan in Borneo

In Borneo the Allies secure the oilfields but do not attempt to clear the whole island of Japanese

OKINAWA

● **June 4** US Marines go ashore on the Oroku Peninsula and secure it in 10 days

● **June 18** General Buckner, commander of US Tenth Army, is killed, highest ranking officer in the US Army to die during the war

● **July 4** British agree to the use of the atomic bomb

June 17 ● US forces face the Yuza Dake – Yaeju Dake escarpment

● **June 21** US forces reach the southern tip of the island. The only opposition now left consists of isolated pockets

Aug 8 ● Russia declares war on Japan at midnight

Aug 9 ● Russian armies invade Manchuria (Manchukuo) under Marshal Vasilievsky

Aug 10–11 ● The Trans-Baikal Front crosses the Hsingan Mountains but is then delayed by fuel and supply problems

Aug 11 ● Russians invade Sakhalin

A constant problem for the Russians is logistics and resupplying their rapidly advancing columns with fuel and food

Aug 20 ● Russians secure Mukden

Aug 18 ● Russians invade Shumshu island in the Kuriles

Aug 4 ● Japanese Taungoo offensive repulsed

Aug 21 ● Russians take Ch'ang-ch'un

Aug 15 ● Emperor Hirohito broadcasts to the Japanese, speaking in public for the first time, telling them of the surrender

● **July 30** USS *Indianapolis* is sunk. Because of communications mishaps, the Navy do not know this. Of 850–900 crew only 316 survive

MANCHURIA

● **Aug 10** The Second Far East Front attacks unopposed across the Amur River from the north

● **Aug 11-16** Russians take Mu-tan-chiang, key position in the east, after a see-saw battle

● **Aug 18** Russians take Hailar, bypassed during the rapid advance of Trans-Baikal Front

● **Aug 19** Russian airborne landings at Mukden and Kirin. Fighting continues despite the official surrender of Japan

● **Aug 18** Russian airborne landing at Harbin

● **Aug 19** Japanese commander in Manchukuo, General Yamada, surrenders, effective next day. But the Soviet advance does not stop and fighting continues

● **Aug 22** Russian airborne landings at Port Arthur and Dairen

● **Aug 24** Russians' armoured spearheads reach Port Arthur

● **Sept 3** Russians secure the Kuriles

● **Aug 25** Russians secure Sakhalin, taking the capital, Toyahara. Over 100,000 refugees make it across the Soya Strait to Japan

● **Sept 9** Allied landings in Mala

● **Aug 22** Pu Yi, last emperor of China, is captured by the Russians. He has been Japan's puppet ruler of Manchukuo

THE ATOMIC BOMBS

● **Aug 6** US B-29 'Enola Gay' drops uranium bomb 'Little Boy' on Hiroshima, destroying 4.2 square miles and killing 80,000 people

● **Aug 9** US B-29 'Bock's Car' drops plutonium bomb 'Fat Man' on Nagasaki, killing 35,000 people

● **Aug 10** Emperor Hirohito tells his government that the Allies' Potsdam surrender terms must be accepted

● **Aug 14** Emperor Hirohito orders surrender according to the Allied terms, while a coup d'etat is being plotted by hardline officers. Formal acceptance is sent

● **Sept 2** Japan makes formal surrende aboard US battleship *Missouri* in Tokyo This day becomes VJ Day

● **Sept 12** British theatre commander Admiral Mountbat takes formal surrender of Japa in Singapore and South-East A

● **Sept 8** General MacArthur arrives in Japan

A veteran of World War I, Austrian born Adolf Hitler joined the German Workers' Party in 1919, later renaming it the National Socialist German Workers' Party (Nazi Party). By 1921 he was its leader and in 1923 he led an unsuccessful *putsch* to overthrow the German Weimar Republic, for which he served a very short prison sentence. The Nazi party steadily grew and as a result of the election of 1933 Hitler was made Chancellor of Germany. Within eighteen months he had suspended the constitution and suppressed all political opposition, giving himself total dictatorial powers. He transformed the German economy to meet the needs of war. His very aggressive foreign policy led to the annexation of Austria and Czechoslovakia before the war and then invasion of Poland, which started World War II. His racial policies were brutal, concentration camps being built to house those he considered racially impure as well as any political opponents. He achieved remarkable military success early in the war and he increasingly believed in his own invincibility, but by 1942 the tide was turning. His dream of

HITLER	
Dates	1889–1945
Background	Austrian; World War I soldier
Offices	The Leader of the Nazi Party; Chancellor of Germany; Fuhrer

Lebensraum (living space) for the German people was the reasoning for the invasion of the USSR which was ultimately responsible for his downfall. His decisions led to the destruction of the German forces at Stalingrad: his refusal to allow them to retreat regardless of cost proved disastrous. As the war progressed his health began to deteriorate. He became increasingly unrealistic with regard to the military forces available to Germany, at the end deploying units which existed only on paper. There was an unsuccessful assassination attempt by Army officers in July 1944. At the end, Hitler committed suicide along with his mistress Eva Braun in April 1945 in his bunker in Berlin as the Russian were battling for the city.

Hitler at a Nazi rally

Winston Churchill

On the outbreak of World War II Churchill was appointed First Lord of the Admiralty. When Germany invaded and took Norway it was a major setback for the British Prime Minister Chamberlain. There was a vote of censure and Chamberlain resigned, and on May 10, 1940, Churchill was appointed prime minister. He then formed a coalition government, including the leaders of the opposition in key positions. Churchill developed a strong personal relationship with Franklin D. Roosevelt. The 'Lend-Lease' agreement of March 1941 allowed Britain to 'borrow' or acquire war materials and weapons on credit from the US. He kept the morale of the British people high even though during the first three years the war it continued to go badly for Britain. He would regularly broadcast to the people whenever a serious situation

CHURCHILL	
Dates	1874–1965
Background	Soldier; politician
Offices	Major cabinet offices; Prime Minister

arose, providing them with inspiration. He was a brilliant orator and a great source of strength to people. There were two votes of no confidence in Parliament against his leadership and they were both overwhelmingly defeated. He did have a tendency to meddle in military matters and sometimes his judgement can be called into question – as with the Greek expedition in 1941, which greatly weakened Allied forces fighting in North Africa. When the USA entered the war he worked even closer with Roosevelt to ensure victory over both Germany and Japan. He always treated his ally Stalin with suspicion, and he was vindicated during the postwar years, but even so the Allies did successfully develop a united strategy against the Axis powers. There was strong pressure from Stalin to land Allied troops in France during 1943, but Churchill rightly insisted on delay, the D-Day landings not taking place until June 6, 1944. Even though highly regarded and much loved by the British people, who looked to Churchill as the wartime leader they needed, the July 1945 election resulted in the Labour leader, Attlee, winning a landslide victory: Churchill was voted out. He was probably the greatest and most inspirational British prime minister of the twentieth century.

One of the greatest of the American presidents, Franklin Delano Roosevelt was elected four times to the office. When Hitler attacked Poland, he tried to make American military aid available to Britain and France as well as taking measures to build up the US armed forces, even though there was strong isolationist opposition to this. After the fall of France the draft for military service was introduced. Roosevelt signed the 'Lend-Lease' bill in March 1941 so that the US could provide aid to Great Britain, Roosevelt seeing the United States as the 'arsenal of democracy'. Four days after the Japanese attacked Pearl Harbor on December 7, 1941, Germany and Italy declared war on the United States. Roosevelt took an active role in choosing the top US military commanders and worked very closely with them on wartime strategy. 'The Declaration of the United Nations,' was made on January 1, 1942, whereby Roosevelt moved to create a grand alliance against the Axis powers: all nations at war with the Axis agreed not to make a separate peace and pledged themselves to

ROOSEVELT	
Dates	1882–1945
Background	Democratic Party politician
Offices	President of the USA and Commander-in-Chief of the US Armed Forces

what was to become the UN. In early 1944 he was given a full medical examination which found serious heart and circulatory problems. Never truly well, he had contracted poliomyelitis in 1921 and had never regained the full use of his legs. The stress and the strain of the war was wearing him out and on April 12, 1945, he suffered a massive stroke, dying within a few hours without regaining consciousness. He was 63 years old. His death came within weeks of the victory in Europe and within months of that over Japan.

Roosevelt seated between Stalin and Churchill at the Yalta Conference in 1945

2 Mussolini, Tojo and Hirohito

WHO WAS WHO Italy/Japan

On June 10, 1940, the fascist **Benito Mussolini** of Italy declared war on Britain and France in alliance with Germany. In North Africa Italy was getting the worst of the combat until the Germans intervened, and the same was true in Greece. In June 1941 he declared war on the Soviet Union and the United States. He was deposed in June 1943 and arrested. He was rescued by the Germans several months later. Little more than a puppet of Germany, he then set up a fascist state in northern Italy. On April 27, 1945, he was arrested by Italian partisans, along with his mistress, and on the next day they were both executed. Their bodies were hung, upside down, in a Milan square beside those of other fascists.

MUSSOLINI

Dates	1883–1945
Background	Journalist; World War I soldier
Offices	The leader of the Fascist Party; Italian dictator, *Il Duce*

Hideki Tojo held extreme right-wing views and was a supporter of Nazi Germany. He became Prime Minister of Japan in October 1941. After failing to reach agreement with the USA, he ordered the attack on Pearl Harbor on December 7, 1941. The war went went well for Japan for the first six months. Later, however, Tojo realised that Japan would not win the war, and he resigned from office when Saipan was lost in July 1944. He attempted suicide by shooting himself in the chest in order to avoid arrest by the US military in 1945. He survived and was tried as a war criminal. Hideki Tojo was executed for war crimes on December 23, 1948.

The Japanese **Emperor Hirohito** reluctantly supported the war against China and the invasion of Manchuria

TOJO

Dates	1884–1948
Background	Professional soldier
Offices	Prime Minister; Minister of War; Home Minister; Foreign Minister; Commander-in-Chief of the General Staff.

in 1937 and approved the attack on Pearl Harbor. With the loss of Okinawa in 1945, Hirohito wanted to seek a negotiated settlement with the Allies. His government refused. After

HIROHITO

Dates	1901–1989
Background	Grandson of the great reforming Emperor Meiji
Offices	Emperor from 1926

the destruction of Hiroshima and Nagasaki Hirohito called a meeting of the Japanese Supreme Council. They wanted to continue the fight but Hirohito intervened. The people of Japan heard the Emperor's voice for the first time on August 15 when he announced Japan's unconditional surrender and the end of the war. Many wanted him to be tried as a war criminal but the head of the occupation forces General MacArthur, refused, believing that Japan would be easier to rule if Hirohito remained.

Mussolini   *Tojo*   *Hirohito*

Joseph Stalin

In 1937 seven of the top Red Army commanders were charged with conspiracy against Stalin and were convicted and executed. Another 30,000 members of the armed forces were also executed, including half of all the army officers. This was all instigated by Stalin's paranoia. He secretly agreed to partition Poland in September 1939 and then conquered Lithuania, Latvia and Estonia and incorporated them into the Soviet Union. Resistance was short-lived and brutally repressed. People from the military, commercial, professional or cultured classes were generally imprisoned or executed. Stalin then suffered a disastrous setback when the Soviets invaded Finland and came up against the dogged resistance of the Finns. Stalin was reluctant to believe the rumours of Germany's impending invasion of the Soviet Union in 1941, calculating that it would not happen until 1942. His military experience was limited, and showed itself, so he turned to the generals he could trust. Stalin's forte was political negotiation. He showed great cunning in his dealings with Roosevelt and Churchill. His constant urging for a second front created some friction within the Allies.

STALIN	
Dates	1879–1953
Background	Bolshevik Revolutionary
Offices	Dictator of the USSR and Commander of the USSR's Armed Forces

By means of commisars Stalin made it very clear to Soviet soldiers who might be thought to have let down the Soviet Union that they would be severely punished. He extended this rule after the war to Soviet soldiers who had been captured: they were to be considered traitors. The Soviet people lived in fear of both Stalin and Hitler and thus had no option but to stand and fight. As the war progressed and the Soviet armies advanced west, the countries that came under Stalin's control would continue to remain so. They were not liberated, they were conquered. Political opposition to Stalin was not tolerated, and this was to lead to the forty years of the 'Cold War'.

Stalin arrives for the Yalta Conference in 1945

Göring and Goebbels

A World War I fighter ace, **Hermann Göring** became an early member of the Nazi party and when Hitler came to power he was made German Air Minister and Prime Minister of Prussia. He created, and until 1936, was the head of, the Gestapo, and he also created and led the Luftwaffe. In 1939 Hitler designated him as his successor. He was responsible for the air war waged by Germany. However, he failed to stop the escape of the British and French troops at Dunkirk and he totally misjudged the RAF during the Battle of Britain. He promised to be able to keep the German troops trapped at Stalingrad supplied by air – another policy decision that completely failed. As the Allied air forces began to win the air war and lay Germany waste, Hitler deprived him of all formal authority in 1943 and then dismissed him shortly before the war ended. He surrendered to American forces and was the chief defendant at the Nuremberg trials. He defended himself with dignity but was convicted and sentenced to death. However, he committed suicide by taking a poison capsule hidden within a false tooth two hours before his scheduled hanging.

GÖRING	
Dates	1893–1946
Background	World War I fighter pilot
Offices	Reich Marshal; C-in-C Luftwaffe; Prussian Minister of Interior

Joseph Goebbels could not serve during World War I as he was disabled with a club foot. He joined the Nazi Party in 1924 and by 1929 he was in overall charge of the Nazi's propaganda machine – a position in which he excelled. When Hitler came to power Goebbels was appointed Minister of Enlightenment and Propaganda, a post he held until 1945. He controlled all aspects of communication, the

GOEBBELS	
Dates	1897–1945
Background	Doctorate of Philosophy
Offices	Minister of Propaganda and Public Enlightenment

Press, radio, publishing, cinema and theatre. He was behind such impressive propaganda films as *Triumph of the Will*, which extolled the racial and athletic virtues of Nazi Germany during the 1936 Olympics. The great Nazi rallies at Nuremberg, even by today's standards of complexity and size, were major organisational achievements. During World War II, when it seemed that all was going Germany's way, it was easy for Goebbels to persuade the public that things were fine. However, after the defeat at the Battle of Stalingrad this was becoming increasingly difficult, although even in the face of the destruction of Germany's cities the morale of the Germans did not collapse. In 1944 he was appointed Reich Commissioner for Total Mobilisation, conscripting women and cutting back on education and entertainment. He was the only senior Nazi leader to stay with Hitler to the end in his bunker as the Battle for Berlin raged above them in April/May 1945. He was a witness at Hitler's wedding to Eva Braun. On May 1 he poisoned his six children, shot his wife and then himself.

Göring   Goebbels

Erwin Rommel

2

WHO WAS WHO Germany

Rommel, who saw military service during World War I, was perceived by the Allies as an honourable opponent of great ability. Personally brave and audacious, he espoused Guderian's *Blitzkrieg* philosophy and was one of the most successful exponents of tank warfare. The 1940 Campaign in the West, saw his 7th 'Ghost' Panzer Division as one of the spearheads of the German advance. An adventurous leader of German and Italian forces in North Africa, defeating British formations of far greater strength, he often surprised his enemy by his tactics, reacting quickly to events and attaining the initiative even when attacked. The Battle of Gazala was a masterpiece of daring tank warfare, but at Alam Halfa and First Alamein his resources were insufficient to achieve the decisive victory he sought. Defeat at Alamein was due largely to his inferiority in numbers and *matériel*, but he conducted masterly defensive battles in Tunisia. He strengthened the Atlantic defences, but was unable to persuade Hitler to allow him deploy armoured formations forward which he hoped would defeat the Allies on the beaches. Injured by air attack and then implicated in the July Bomb Plot on Hitler's life, he was forced to take his own life.

ERWIN ROMMEL	
Rank attained	Generalfeldmarschall (1942)
Dates	1894–1944
Background	Career soldier; Berlin Military Academy; awarded *Pour le Mérite* in World War I; wrote *Enemy Attack!* treatise on infantry tactics 1927
Commands	Hitler's personal body-guard 1933–37; 7th Panzer Division during Campaign in the West; Afrika Korps (later Panzer Armee Afrika) 1941–43; advisory command Italy 1943–44; command of troops on Western Front (France/Belgium) 1944
Campaigns	West 1940; Africa 1941–44; Normandy 1944
Battles	Two successful offensives in the Western Desert 1941–42; Gazala 1942; took Tobruk 1942; Alam Halfa and two Battles of El Alamein 1942; Kasserine Pass 1943; Mareth Line 1943; Tunisia 1943; Normandy 1944

Rommel's Afrika Korps Mk IV tanks pass a knocked-out British Bren Gun Carrier

29

GUDERIAN

Rank attained	General
Dates	1888–1954
Background	Career soldier; Metz War School; wrote *Achtung Panzer!* treatise on tank tactics, 1937
Commands	XIX Panzer Corps, 1939–40; 2nd Panzer Group, 1941; Chief of Panzer Command, 1943; Chief of Army General Staff; 1944
Campaigns	Poland, 1939; West, 1940; Russia, 1941

In the 1930s **Heinz Guderian** proposed the revolutionary theory that tanks were the primary weapon, then published a book on the subject. He laid the foundations for the first three Panzer divisions in 1935. The Polish and Western Campaigns of 1939 and 1940 proved the theory of *Blitzkrieg* that he espoused. His ideas worked well in Russia in 1941, where his force, 2nd Panzer Group, captured huge numbers of Soviet soldiers, but his criticism of Hitler's military tactics led to his dismissal in December 1941. For over a year he was not given an appointment, but he was recalled as Inspector of Armoured Troops, making him the chief of the Panzer Command. He was invited to join the July Bomb Plot to kill Hitler, but declined. He was made Chief of the General Staff, but he continued to fall out with Hitler and was forced to take sick leave just a month or so before the end of the war.

The son of a Prussian aristocrat, **Erich von Manstein** is considered as one of the ablest of the German generals during World War II. After he was wounded in World War I he served as a staff officer. He was von Rundstedt's Chief of Staff during the Polish Campaign in 1939. His inspired ideas

for the campaign in the West were adopted by Hitler, even though opposed by Field Marshal von Brauchitsch, the Commander-in-Chief and General Halder, the Chief of Staff. The ensuing conquest of France was a military triumph during which Manstein commanded XXXVIII Corps. In Russia his Eleventh Army defeated the Soviets in the Crimea. During the Battle of Stalingrad he almost managed to relieve the Sixth Army trapped there. Then, commanding Army Group South in a counter-offensive, he won a major victory at Kharkov. After the German defeat at the Battle of Kursk in 1943 he led his forces through a series of defensive battles as the Germans were pushed back by the Soviets. By March 1944 he had fallen out of favour with Hitler, and as a result he was dismissed and never held another command.

Guderian   Manstein

VON MANSTEIN

Rank attained	Field Marshal
Dates	1887–1973
Background	Career soldier
Commands	XXXVIII Corps, 1940; LVI Panzer Corps, 1941; Eleventh Army, 1941; Army Group Don, 1942; Army Group South, 1943
Campaigns	West, 1940; Russia 1941–44

Kesselring and von Rundstedt

KESSELRING

Rank attained	Field Marshal
Dates	1889–1960
Background	Career soldier, then service with Luftwaffe
Commands	Luftflotte I, 1939; Luftflotte II, 1940; C-in-C South, 1941–45; C-in-C West, 1945
Campaigns	Poland, 1939; Belgium/France, 1940; Battle of Britain, 1940; Russia, 1941; Mediterranean, 1941–45; C-in-C West, 1945

Albert Kesselring served as a army staff officer during World War I. In 1936 he transferred to the Luftwaffe. He commanded Luftflotte I (First Air Fleet) during the Polish campaign and Luftflotte II during the 1940 campaign in the West. His air fleet participated in the Battle of Britain. Luftflotte II was then transferred east for the invasion of Russia. He was appointed C-in-C South in 1941 to establish Axis air dominance over the Mediterranean and was involved with the campaign in the North African desert. He conducted a brilliant defence in Sicily and Italy, always without adequate reserves of men and equipment. In March 1945 Hitler transferred him to take over command in the West but Germany was about to collapse and he negotiated surrender with the Americans. He was found guilty of war crimes but his death sentence was commuted to one of life imprisonment and in 1953 he was released on grounds of ill health.

The aristocratic Prussian, **Gerd von Rundstedt** served as a staff officer during World War I. He retired in 1938 but was brought back to help plan the invasion of Poland. He commanded Army Group A that led the attack in the West and the fall of France. Promoted to Field Marshal in July 1940, he was to command the aborted invasion of Great Britain. He then commanded Army Group South during the invasion of Russia. He was dismissed by Hitler in November 1941 for withdrawing against orders. He was recalled for active service in March 1942, becoming C-in-C West. He clashed with Rommel over how to defeat the expected invasion. He conducted a skilled defence in the West and is considered one of the outstanding German commanders of the war. Hitler dismissed him again in March 1945. He was to be put on trial for war crimes but ill health saved him.

VON RUNDSTEDT

Rank attained	Field Marshal
Dates	1875–1953
Background	Career soldier, Kriegsakademie, Berlin
Commands	Army Group South, 1939; C-in-C South, 1939; Army Group South, 1939; C-in-C West, 1940; Army Group South, 1941; C-in-C West; 1942
Campaigns	Poland, 1939; France, 1940; Russia, 1941; The West, 1942–44

Kesselring   *von Rundstedt*

Bernard Montgomery

After being wounded in World War I in 1914, Montgomery served as a staff officer. An ascetic man, he was a master of detail. He commanded the 3rd Division during the Battle of France in 1940. For the next two years he concentrated on army training. In the late summer of 1942 he was appointed to command the Eighth Army in North Africa. His victory at the Battle of El Alamein in October 1942 was one of the turning points of the war, although, during the follow-up to the battle, he was accused by some of letting the remainder of the Axis forces slip away after the battle. Cornered between Montgomery with the Eighth Army and Allied forces from the 'Torch' landings in the west, the Axis forces surrendered in May 1943. He then commanded the British forces during the invasion of Sicily and the landings in southern Italy and was transferred back to the UK in December 1943 to help plan for the landings in Normandy. His influence and organisational skills came to the fore in this crucial planning stage, contributing in no small measure to the success of the landings. After commanding the landings of June 6, 1944 he commanded the British and Canadian forces in their drive across Belgium and Holland and north-west Germany, taking the final surrender there on 4 May 1945.

MONTGOMERY	
Rank attained	Field Marshal
Dates	1887–1976
Background	Career soldier; Sandhurst Military Academy; wounded in 1914
Commands	3th Division during Campaign in France, 1940; UK 5th and then 12th Corps, 1940–41; South-Eastern Command 1941–42; Eighth Army 1942–43; 21st Army Group 1944–45
Campaigns	France, 1940; North Africa 1942–43; Sicily 1943; Italy 1943; North-West Europe, 1944–45
Battles	2nd El Alamein 1942; Mareth Line, 1943; Normandy, 1944, Arnhem, 1944; Rhine 1945

Montgomery was an egocentric and conceited man, and many found it difficult to work with him, but he was able to communicate with the ordinary soldiers under his command, instilling them with his own self-confidence.

Montgomery (left) with HM King George VI

SLIM

Rank attained	Field Marshal
Dates	1891–1970
Background	Career soldier, enlisted as a private
Commands	5th Indian Division, 1940; 10th Indian Division, 1941; I Burma Corps, 1942; XVIII Corps, 1943; 14th Army, 1943
Campaigns	Sudan, 1940; Syria/Iraq/Iran, 1941; Burma/India, 1942–45

In 1914 at the beginning of World War I, **Bill Slim** enlisted as a private soldier; he eventually became a Field Marshal. He transferred to the Indian Army in 1919. He commanded two Indian Divisions, seeing active service in Sudan, Syria, Iraq and Iran before going to Burma in 1942 and taking command of the 1st Burma Corps. As he arrived, British forces were retreating the 900 miles from Rangoon into India. He built up the morale of XVIII Corps and then took command of the 14th Army and launched an offensive into Burma in December 1943. In 1944 he defeated an impressive Japanese counter-attack at the Battle of Imphal/Kohima in India, inflicting 50,000 casualties on them. By 1945 his troops had fought all the way back to Rangoon, defeating the Japanese Army in Burma. He had achieved one of the greatest land victories over the Japanese, inflicting nearly 350,000 casualties on them. An experienced soldier, Slim was greatly liked and admired as a military commander. He inspired confidence and was held in great affection by his men.

Sir Archibald Wavell was a well-respected soldier whose military career began during the Boer War. He lost an eye fighting in World War I. During 1940–41 he defeated the Italians in North and East Africa, capturing 110,000 troops. In March 1941, after these successes, the best of his military units were sent to the Balkans during the ill-fated attempt to help the Greeks, at the same time as Rommel was striking into Libya. Wavell was forced into retreat as trouble also flared in Iraq and Syria. His offensives against Rommel in May and June 1941 came to naught. He was then transferred to India as C-in-C. His defeat in Burma by the Japanese was followed by his failed counter-offensives in 1942. He was promoted to Field Marshal and given the political post of Viceroy of India. Always under-resourced and pressured by London, this talented general was poorly used.

WAVELL

Rank attained	Field Marshal
Dates	1883–1950
Background	Career soldier; Sandhurst Military Academy, wounded in WWI
Commands	C-in-C Middle East Command, 1939–41; C-in-C India, 1941–43
Campaigns	North Africa, 1939–41; East Africa, 1940; Greece, 1941; Syria/Iraq/Iran,1941; Burma, 1943

Slim   Wavell

Wingate and Crerar

WINGATE

Rank attained	Major General
Dates	1903–44
Background	Career soldier, Royal Military Academy, Woolwich
Commands	'Gideon Force', Ethiopia, 1941; 'Chindits', Burma 1942–44
Campaigns/ Battles	Palestine, 1936; Ethiopia, 1940–41; Burma, 1942–44

Wingate   Crerar

Orde Wingate was born in India. He had a background of guerrilla fighting in pre-war Palestine, and while commanding 'Gideon Force' he assisted the Ethiopians in their successful revolt against the Italians. After a period of illness and a desk job he went to the Far East to form what was to be known as the 'Chindits', brigade-sized units specialising in unconventional warfare that would operate behind Japanese lines in Burma. The Chindits had limited success in 1943 but Wingate became a popular hero. In 1944 they fought against the Japanese in an air-dropped expedition into Burma but Wingate died in an air crash in the jungle before the outcome of the expedition was settled. The operation

was a success but success was achieved at a high price in terms of casualties. A very religious man, Wingate had a moody personality with a fanatical quality that could get men to attempt the impossible.

Having served with distinction during World War I, General **Henry Crerar** was appointed Chief of the Canadian Staff in 1941. He commanded the 1 Canadian Corps during the Italian Campaign and then was appointed to command the 1st Canadian Army for the invasion of Normandy. In late 1944 he took command of the largest military force ever led by a Canadian – some 500,000 men, consisting of 13 divisions made up of Canadians, Britons, Americans, Belgians, Dutchmen and Poles. There were tensions between him and General Montgomery, his commanding officer. Not a charismatic man, he was not well known for inspiring his men, but he was a very proficient planner and administrator. He had the good fortune of having as his second-in-command the inspirational and inventive Lieutenant General Simonds. Crerar was the 'executive' commander of the 1st Canadian Army and Simonds the battlefield commander.

CRERAR

Rank attained	General
Dates	1888–1965
Background	Career soldier; Royal Military College, Kingston, Canada
Commands	Chief of the Canadian General Staff, 1941; 2nd Canadian Division, 1942–43; I Canadian Corps, 1942–44; C-in-C First Canadian Army; 1944–45
Campaigns/ Battles	Italy, 1943; North-West Europe, 1943–45

Dwight D. Eisenhower

At the age of 28 this popular, out-going Texan was given the task of forming the US Army's first tank corps during World War I. From the Operations Branch in Washington he was sent to Great Britain in 1942 to lead the American staff there. He was a good choice in achieving the harmony needed within the Allied Forces' HQ. He commanded the invasion of French North Africa in November 1942. He was promoted to four-star general in February 1943. In December 1943 he was appointed as Supreme Commander in the Mediterranean theatre of operations. Then, in January 1944, he was appointed as the Supreme Commander of the Allied Expeditionary Forces for the invasion of Europe. He was not a fighting general in the mould of Patton or Bradley but, as President Roosevelt believed, the best politician among any of the military commanders – which was exactly what the job called for. He did, however, insist on the 'broad front' strategy instead of the 'narrow front' as urged by Montgomery and Patton. The narrow front strategy might have ended the war earlier with powerful, deep thrusts into German territory, making for Berlin, while the broader front was the slower but less risky option. He ended the war being looked upon as a hero, as much by the British as by the Americans. After the war he went on to be twice elected US President.

EISENHOWER

Rank attained	General of the Army
Dates	1890–1969
Background	Career soldier; West Point Military Academy
Commands	Operations Division, 1942; US Commanding General, European Theatre of Operations, 1942; Supreme Allied Command, Europe. 1943–45
Campaigns	North Africa, 1942–43; Sicily 1943; Italy 1943; North-West Europe, 1943–45

Eisenhower (centre)

Douglas MacArthur

One of the most controversial generals of the US Army, Douglas MacArthur was the son of an army officer from a distinguished family. He graduated from West Point with the highest marks ever received. After service in World War I he rose rapidly through the ranks to become Army Chief of Staff. He retired in 1937, becoming a field marshal with the Philippine Army. In 1941 he was recalled to US service by Roosevelt.

After his unsuccessful defence of the Philippines he escaped to Australia in March 1942, promising, 'I shall return'. From there he began the conquest of the South-West Pacific, island-hopping all the way to the retaking of the Philippines in 1945. He had the honour of accepting the Japanese formal surrender in Tokyo Bay. He was idolised by the American public but disliked by Roosevelt and by most of the other top-ranking military men. He loved publicity and he was flamboyant, vain and egotistical. He had a total contempt for criticism and many of those who had authority over him. He was, however, charming and gracious and a bold leader with great imagination. Like a potentate, he ruled post-war Japan but the Korean War led to his downfall.

MACARTHUR	
Rank attained	General
Dates	1880–1964
Background	Career soldier; West Point Military Academy
Commands	Commander of US Forces in the Far East, 1941; South-West Pacific Area, 1942; US Army Forces in the Pacific, 1945
Campaigns	Philippines, 1941–42; New Guinea and the Solomons, 1942–44; Philippines, 1945

MacArthur signs the Japanese surrender, Tokyo Bay

George S. Patton

Nicknamed 'Old Blood and Guts', Patton came from a Californian family with a strong military background and he always wanted to be a soldier. He fought in the Mexican Campaign of 1916 and in World War I, when he was assigned to tanks. Between the wars he reverted to the old horsed cavalry. In 1940 he commanded a brigade of the newly-formed 2nd Armored Division and later that year, after pro-motion to Major General, the command of the whole division and then the 1st Armored Corps.

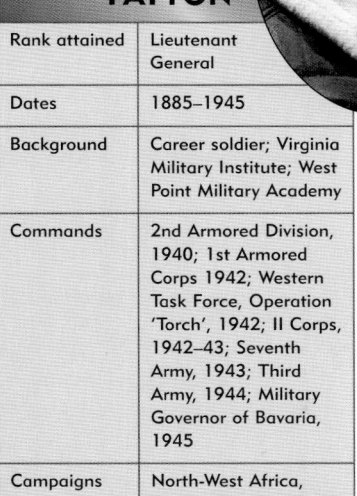

In November 1942 he commanded the Western Task Force that successfully landed in French Morocco. In the Sicilian Campaign he commanded the US Seventh Army. Unfortunately two incidents occurred in which he accused soldiers of cowardice because they were suffering from combat fatigue. This was reported in the press and he was relieved of command for eleven months as a con-sequence. In January 1944 he was given command of the US Third Army. He launched a series of armoured thrusts from Normandy across France to the German border. He then relieved the besieged town of Bastogne during the Battle of the Bulge. In March 1945 his forces drove deep into Germany, Austria and Czechoslovakia at the war's end. He was promoted to four-star general in April 1945. He was hailed as the outstanding American general of the war, a flamboyant, aggressive and meticulous commander, deeply religious and widely read. He died in a car accident in December 1945.

Infantrymen of Patton's 10th Infantry Battalion, Third Army, in action

PATTON	
Rank attained	Lieutenant General
Dates	1885–1945
Background	Career soldier; Virginia Military Institute; West Point Military Academy
Commands	2nd Armored Division, 1940; 1st Armored Corps 1942; Western Task Force, Operation 'Torch', 1942; II Corps, 1942–43; Seventh Army, 1943; Third Army, 1944; Military Governor of Bavaria, 1945
Campaigns	North-West Africa, 1942–43; Sicily 1943; North West Europe, 1943–45

BRADLEY	
Rank attained	General
Dates	1893–1981
Background	Career soldier; West Point Military Academy
Commands	82nd and 28th Divisions, 1942; II Corps, 1943; First Army, 1943; Twelfth Army Group, 1944;
Campaigns	North Africa, 1943; Sicily, 1943; North-West Europe, 1943–45

Bradley   Stilwell

Omar Bradley taught at West Point before the war and later served on the General Staff. Early in 1942 he commanded and trained the 82nd and 28th Divisions in the United States Army. He was then transferred to North Africa as deputy to General Patton in II Corps. Bradley took over command when Patton left, leading the corps through the remainder of the North African Campaign, capturing Bizerta and taking 40,000 prisoners. He then led his corps in Sicily. He left II Corps and took command of the First Army in Great Britain prior to the invasion of France. He commanded the US forces at D-Day and led the First Army in France until taking command of the 12th Army Group which consisted of four armies, a post that he held until the end of the war. During the Battle of the Bulge he behaved with great coolness, stemming a German breakthrough. His men then sealed the Ruhr Pocket, capturing 335,000 enemy soldiers. He was promoted to a full general in March 1945. At the end of the war he commanded more men than any other US general in history – 1,300,000. A man of common sense, he was highly regarded by those who served under him, nicknaming him the 'GI's General'. Eisenhower thought that he was the best of the battlefield commanders.

General **'Vinegar Joe' Stilwell** was a cantankerous and difficult man to work with – hence his nickname. An anglophobe, he had an implacable dislike of the British. He served in World War I, had two tours of duty in China before the war and was the US military attaché in Peking from 1935 to 1939. He was sent to China in 1942 as Chiang Kai-shek's chief of staff and the commander of the Chinese Fifth and Sixth Armies. He was driven from Burma by the Japanese but returned in 1943. Friction between him and Chiang over troop deployments resulted in his withdrawal from the theatre of operations in 1944. He then went on to command the US Tenth Army during the battle for Okinawa.

STILWELL	
Rank attained	General
Dates	1883–1946
Background	Career soldier; West Point Military Academy
Commands	Commander US Forces China, 1942; Chinese Fifth and Sixth Armies, 1942; Deputy South-East Asia Command, 1943; Tenth Army, 1945
Campaigns	Burma/China, 1942–44; Okinawa, 1945

ZHUKOV

Rank attained	Marshal
Dates	1896–1974
Background	Career soldier, NCO in Tsarist Army; Red Army, 1918
Commands	Leningrad Front, 1941; West Front, 1941–42; West Theatre, 1942–45
Campaigns/ Battles	Mongolia, 1939; Leningrad, 1941; Moscow, 1941–42; Stalingrad, 1942–43; Kursk, 1943; Poland, 1944; Berlin, 1945

Georgi Zhukov was the son of a peasant, serving in the Imperial Russian Army during World War I before joining the Red Army. When commanding the Soviet forces in Mongolia he defeated the Japanese Kwantung Army. In 1941 he became the Soviet Chief of the General Staff. In July 1941 he was posted to the armies east of Moscow. He was ordered to take command at Leningrad. He then returned to Moscow, counterattacking the Germans on December 6, 1941. Named Deputy Supreme Commander, he played a part in defeating the Germans at Stalingrad. The victory at Kursk merged into the Soviet Summer Offensive, when he co-ordinated the

First and Second Ukrainian Fronts in the drive west. Zhukov personally took command of the First Ukrainian Front when its commander was wounded in February 1944. He helped to co-ordinate Operation 'Bagration', the summer offensive in 1944, in which the Soviets destroyed the Germans' Army Group Centre. In November he was put in command of the First Belorussian Front, which had the most direct approach to Berlin. With the fall of Berlin he became the most celebrated of all the Soviet Marshals.

Second only to Marshal Zhukov, **Ivan Konev** displayed great capability in handling armies. During the Battle of Moscow he commanded the Kalinin Front in the supporting, but decisive, struggle on the northern flank at the time of the battle. He became prominent at the Battle of Kursk, and during the 1943–44 offensives he played a prominent part in the Soviets' advance west. He led the one million men of the First Ukrainian Front that fought the Battle of Berlin. His forces played a prominent part in the envelopment of the city and then the final victory. Three days after this his forces then advanced south and entered Prague.

KONEV

Rank attained	Marshal
Dates	1897–1973
Background	Career soldier; military commissar during Russian Civil War; Funz Military Academy
Commands	Kalinin Front, 1941; West Front, 1942; Steppe Front, 1943; Second Ukrainian Front, 1943; First Ukrainian Front, 1944
Campaigns/ Battles	Moscow, 1941; Kursk, 1943; Berlin, 1945

Zhukov   *Konev*

Yamashita and Imamura

Yamashita   Imamura

YAMASHITA	
Rank attained	General
Dates	1884–1946
Background	Career soldier, Kainan Middle School
Commands	C-in-C 25th Army, 1941; C-in-C 14th Army, 1944

IMAMURA	
Rank attained	General
Dates	1886–1968
Background	Career soldier, graduated from Japanese War College
Commands	5th Division, 1938; Inspector of Military Training, 1940; 23rd Army, 1941; 8th Area Army, 1942

Out the outbreak of the Pacific War, General **Tomoyuki Yamashita**, the 'Tiger of Malaya', with only 36,000 men, defeated 100,000 British Empire troops in capturing Malaya and Singapore – all within ten weeks. He was one of the most formidable Japanese generals of World War II. In November 1941 he had taken command of the 25th Army. A first rate strategist, he trained his troops in the techniques of jungle warfare as well as helping to conceive the plan for the invasion of the Malay peninsula. In the course of the campaign, Yamashita's troops overran all of Malaya and captured Singapore on February 15, 1942. He did not see active service again until 1944, when he took command of the 14th Army for the defence of the Philippines. His forces were defeated in both the Leyte and the Luzon campaigns, but he held out until after the surrender was announced from Tokyo in August 1945, not ceding to the Americans until September 3, 1945. He was charged with war crimes because of the atrocities his troops committed while under his command in the Philippines which had resulted in the deaths of 100,000 people. He was convicted and hanged in Manila in 1946.

Hitoshi Imamura, a lieutenant-general, commanded the 5th Division in China from 1938–40. He was Inspector General of Military Education from 1940 until 1941. He became Commander of the 16th Army in late 1941, leading it during the Dutch East Indies Campaign of 1942 and landing in Java. He had to abandon the ship he was on after it had been accidentally torpedoed by a Japanese cruiser, having to leap into the sea. He then commanded 8th Area Army in late 1942 which was responsible for the whole of the south-east Pacific, his HQ being at Rabaul, New Britain. He adopted quite a liberal regime, using a minimum of force while establishing order. He was promoted to full general in 1943. As the Allies went on the offensive they began to encroach on his area of command. New Britain became isolated as islands were lost to the Allies. He had to send 6,500 of his troops to reinforce two of the New Guinea islands but their transports were sunk and most of the men were lost. At the end of the war, he was the signatory to the surrender of all Japanese forces in the area. He was also a representative at the surrender of Singapore. He was subsequently tried for war crimes and imprisoned from 1946 to 1954.

Cavallero and Iachino 2

WHO WAS WHO Italy

CAVALLERO

Rank attained	Marshal
Dates	1880–1943
Background	Career soldier, Modena Military School
Commands	C-in-C East Africa, 1938; Comando Supremo, 1940; C-in-C Greece, 1940; C-in-C General Staff, 1941

Cavallero

Iachino

IACHINO

Rank attained	Admiral
Dates	1889–1976
Background	Career sailor
Commands	Cruiser Force, 1940; C-in-C Italian Fleet, 1940–43

Count Ugo Cavallero served successfully during World War I and became the Supreme Commander of the Italian Armed Forces in East Africa in 1938. He took over as Chief of Comando Supremo on December 6, 1940. He also became Commander of Italian forces fighting against Greece on December 30, 1940. After the Italian occupation of Greece, he returned to Italy. He then became Chief of General Staff of the three armed forces. He was a friend of General Kesselring. He was promoted to Field Marshal in 1942. After the defeats in Russia and the loss of Libya, Cavallero was removed from the Comando Supremo in 1943, and following Mussolini's fall in the same year he was arrested. The Italian King set him free, but he was re-arrested along with many fascist leaders. He wrote a memorandum claiming he was an anti-fascist and that he had plotted against Mussolini. With the Italian surrendered in 1943, the Germans took him as they wanted to give him command of the remaining Italian forces loyal to the Germans but the SS obtained the memorandum that he had written earlier and they surmised that he was an anti-fascist. Cavallero committed suicide on September 14, 1943, probably at the Germans' instigation.

The highly regarded Admiral **Angelo Iachino** became C-in-C of the Italian Fleet in December 1940, replacing Admiral Campioni a month after the disaster at Taranto. Prior to this promotion he had commanded the Italian cruiser force, which had acquitted itself well in action against the Royal Navy. His ships were always plagued by lack of fuel oil and their lack of sonar and radar. He also had the problem of too much control from the high command in Rome, complaining that they interfered with orders, even down to the minor naval units. He was in his flagship *Vittorio Veneto* commanding the Italian ships at the Battle of Matapan, where they suffered a major defeat. There is no doubt that Iachino was also badly served by his air reconnaissance, and his fleet was hampered by the fact that it did not possess an aircraft carrier to provide constant air cover. As the war progressed, the lack of fuel for his ships increasingly handicapped the ability of his men to train at sea and of his ships to carry out major sorties.

41

Raeder and Dönitz

Raeder   Dönitz

RAEDER

Rank attained	Grand Admiral
Dates	1876–1960
Background	Career sailor
Commands	C-in-C German Navy, 1939–43

DÖNITZ

Rank attained	Grand Admiral
Dates	1891–1980
Background	Career sailor
Commands	Flag Officer Commanding U-Boats, 1935; C-in-C German Navy, 1943

Admiral **Erich Raeder** saw service in World War I and naval action during the Battle of Jutland. He developed the idea of the 'pocket' battleship. Hitler appointed him C-in-C of the German Navy. He was in overall command of the planning of the successful seaborne invasion of Norway, but he thought that the projected invasion of Great Britain in 1940 far too ambitious. Hitler and he always clashed with regard to the use of the German surface fleet. After the failure of German ships during the Battle of the Barents Sea, Hitler threatened to scrap the surface fleet and deploy only U-boats. He then had Raeder dismissed and replaced him with Dönitz. Raeder was sentenced to ten years' imprisonment for war crimes at Nuremberg.

Karl Dönitz also saw service during World War I, including the command of a U-boat. In 1939 he published a monograph *Die U-bootswaffe* (The U-Boat Arm). He developed the tactical concept of the submarine 'wolf pack' wherein a number of submarines would simultaneously attack a convoy at night, on the surface, using their superior surface speed and low silhouette to avoid the escorts. When he received command of the U-Boat Arm he established firm control over the technical aspects of submarine design as well as their tactical use. He started the war with just 57 boats, and even though initially there were problems with German torpedo design the U-boat Arm had some spectacular successes, such as the sinking of the British battleship HMS *Royal Oak* within the confines of the British naval base at Scapa Flow. Between May and December 1940, a period that the U-boat Arm called *'Die Glückliche Zeit'* (The Happy Time), the U-boats operated with a high degree of success considering how few in number they were. A second 'Happy Time' lasted from January to August 1942 with U-boats attacking unprotected US shipping off the east coast of the United States. By 1943 Dönitz had more that 200 U-boats in commission but by then the Allies had got the better of them. It was not impossible that Dönitz could have forced Britain to surrender had he been given sufficient numbers of U-boats earlier in the war. Hitler always held Dönitz in high regard and named him as his successor: he became Head of State on April 30, 1945, negotiating the capitulation. A well-respected leader and highly regarded by both his foes and those that served with him, he was sentenced to ten years' imprisonment at the Nuremberg Trials.

Tovey and Ramsay

2

Tovey   Ramsay

TOVEY

Rank attained	Admiral of the Fleet
Dates	1885–1971
Background	Career sailor, training HMS *Britannia*
Commands	C-in-C Home Fleet, 1940–43; First Sea Lord, 1943

John Tovey entered the Navy as a cadet in January 1900 and served during World War I. Given command of the destroyer HMS *Onslow*, he took part in the Battle of Jutland. During World War II he was a Vice-Admiral and second-in-command of the Mediterranean fleet, leading the action against the Italians off Calabria in July 1940 and ten days later sinking the Italian cruiser *Bartolomeo Colleoni*. At the end of 1940 he was promoted to C-in-C Home Fleet. On May 22,1941 he sailed from Scapa Flow towards the Denmark Strait in an attempt to intercept the German battleship *Bismarck*. On May 24 HMS *Hood* was sunk by *Bismarck*; HMS *Prince of Wales* withdrew, damaged, while Tovey's ships were still 300 miles away. Aircraft from *Ark Royal* of Force H damaged *Bismarck* and effectively stopped the ship. *Bismarck* then faced the com-

bined firepower of Tovey's battleships *King George V* and *Rodney*, and attendant cruisers, sustaining very heavy damage before being sunk by torpedoes from HMS *Dorsetshire*. In 1943 he relinquished the Home Fleet command and became Commander-in-Chief at the Nore, preparing for the Allied invasion of Sicily and then D-Day.

In World War I, **Bertram Ramsay** served in the Grand Fleet and the Dover Patrol. In 1938 he resigned and was put on the retired list but in 1939 he was recalled to take over the Dover Command. With the collapse of the British and French armies in 1940, he was put in charge of the superbly handled Operation 'Dynamo', the evacuation of over 300,000 British and French troops from Dunkirk. An expert in amphibious warfare, Ramsay assisted in the planning of the Algerian landings and was Naval Commander of the Eastern Task Force for the Sicily invasion and later played a major part in the planning and execution of Operation 'Overlord', the D-Day invasion of Europe. He was Chief of Operational Command for the landings. Ramsay's last operation was the Allied attack on Walcheren, the taking of which allowed the port of Antwerp to be used by the Allies. In January 1945, he was killed in an air crash. Eisenhower thought Ramsey an exceptionally able commander. He was a modest but tough man, much admired by his colleagues.

RAMSAY

Rank attained	Admiral
Dates	1883–1945
Background	Career sailor, Naval War College
Commands	Dover Command, 1940; Eastern Task Force, Sicily Invasion, 1943; Allied Expeditionary Force, Normandy Invasion, 1944

WHO WAS WHO Great Britain

Cunningham and Somerville

CUNNINGHAM

Rank attained	Admiral of the Fleet
Dates	1883–1963
Background	Career sailor, training HMS *Britannia*
Commands	C-in-C Mediterranean Fleet, 1939–42; First Sea Lord, 1943

Andrew Cunningham was the very essence of a fighting admiral with the true Nelsonian spirit, once signalling to his ships, 'Sink, burn and destroy: let nothing pass.' He joined the Royal Navy as a cadet in 1897, serving in the Boer War and World War I. He became C-in-C Mediterranean Fleet in 1939. In November 1940 his Fleet Air Arm aircraft sank one battleship and crippled two others in the harbour at Taranto (a precursor of the Pearl Harbor attack). In May 1941 his fleet sank three Italian heavy cruisers and two destroyers and badly damaged a battleship at the Battle of Cape Matapan. During the battle for Crete, even though suffering heavy losses through lack of air cover, his ships managed to rescue 75% of the 22,000 Allied troops trapped on the island. His fleet helped keep the island of Malta supplied during its three-year bombing ordeal and siege. Appointed First Sea Lord, he played a major part in all operations until the war's end. An outstanding commander, he was well liked and respected

by Churchill and Eisenhower but most of all by the seamen who served under his command.

Cunningham   Somerville

Born in New Zealand, **James Somerville** was promoted to Vice-Admiral in 1937 then placed on the retired list in 1939. Returned to active duty after the declaration of war, he was appointed as C-in-C of Force H in 1940. After the fall of France his ships were obliged to attack French warships anchored in the harbour at Mers el-Kébir because the French admiral would not hand over this fleet to continue the fight against the Nazis, and because of the fear that they would fall into the hands of the Germans. One French battleship was sunk, two were heavily damaged and one escaped. In May 1941 Somerville's Force H was in action against *Bismarck*, aircraft from *Ark Royal* inflicting torpedo damage on the German ship and causing the steering problems that led to her being sunk by British warships. As commander of Force H he was instrumental in getting convoys through the Mediterranean in order to keep the British forces in North Africa supplied. He was selected to command the hastily organised British Eastern Fleet in the spring of 1942 after Japan entered the war. Things did not go well at first when Japanese warships sortied into the Indian Ocean sinking one British light carrier, two cruisers and a destroyer before retiring. Later the tables would be turned. In 1945 Somerville became head of the British Naval Mission in Washington.

SOMERVILLE

Rank attained	Admiral
Dates	1882–1949
Background	Career sailor
Commands	Commander of Force H, 1940; Eastern Fleet, 1942

Nimitz and King 2

NIMITZ

Rank attained	Fleet Admiral
Dates	1885–1966
Background	United States Naval Academy, Annapolis
Commands	Pacific Fleet, 1941; C-in-C Naval Operations, 1945

Nimitz   King

WHO WAS WHO USA

Chester Nimitz joined the United States Navy in 1905. During World War I he was chief of staff of the US Atlantic Submarine Force. Promoted to Rear-Admiral in 1938, Nimitz was placed in charge of the Pacific Fleet after the attack on Pearl Harbor. He was a firm believer in an offensive rather than a defensive war and in gaining the initiative over the enemy. He met regularly with Admiral King and General MacArthur, their first objective being to establish a line of communication across the South Pacific to Australia, resulting in the Battle of the Coral Sea. With the aid of excellent intelligence he then planned and executed the decisive US naval victory at the Battle of Midway. He landed forces on the island of Guadalcanal: thus leading to another decisive US victory. Nimitz employed the effective strategy of making a series of amphibious landings on islands across the Central Pacific as a means of approach to the Japanese home islands. He also

fought a number of major naval battles that led to the virtual destruction of the Imperial Japanese Navy, and his submarines gradually eliminated the Japanese merchant marine. An affable but determined man, he was one of the ablest stategists the US Navy has ever produced. The Pacific war was won by his strategy.

Ernest J. King served in the Spanish-American War of 1898 and also during World War I. In February 1941 he was given the rank of Admiral as C-in-C Atlantic Fleet and in December of that year he became C-in-C US Fleet. In 1942 the posts of C-in-C US Fleet and Chief of Naval Operations were combined and Admiral King assumed these combined duties. Throughout the war King and MacArthur constantly disagreed over strategy: MacArthur favoured an early return to the Philippines but King wanted to bypass them and devote all resources to the taking of Formosa, which he believed, could then serve as a base for invading China. Roosevelt resolved the disagreement and MacArthur got his way. A master planner, King formulated the fleet train system which made it possible to keep large numbers of American warships at sea without the need for them to return to base. Single-minded and intolerant, King was nevertheless one of the great naval leaders of the war. In 1944 he was promoted to the newly created rank of Fleet Admiral.

KING

Rank attained	Fleet Admiral
Dates	1892–1956
Background	United States Naval Academy, Annapolis
Commands	C-in-C Atlantic Fleet, 1941; C-in-C US Fleet, 1941

Fletcher and Halsey

FLETCHER

Rank attained	Vice-Admiral
Dates	1885–1973
Background	United States Naval Academy, Annapolis
Commands	Task Force 17, 1942; C-in-C Northern Pacific, 1942

Fletcher   Halsey

Frank Fletcher saw service as a destroyer captain during World War I. In January 1942, as Rear-Admiral Fletcher, he was given command of a carrier task force. He delayed his task force's arrival at Wake Island because of a controversial decision to refuel, resulting in the loss of the island to the Japanese before US naval forces could arrive. He supported the reinforcing of other vital strategic islands in the South Pacific. He then raided Japanese positions in the Central Pacific, New Guinea and the Solomon Islands and turned back the Japanese at the Battle of the Coral Sea. He saw his flagship, the USS *Yorktown*, sink under him at the Battle of Midway. He has been criticised for withdrawing his naval forces too precipitately at the Battle of Guadalcanal leaving the US Marines who were defending the island isolated. At the Battle of the Eastern Solomons he was again criticised for being overcautious. He then became C-in-C Northern Pacific, transporting aid to Russia via the

western route. He remained at this post until the war's end.

During World War I **William 'Bull' Halsey** served in the US Destroyer Force. In 1940 he was the most senior carrier admiral, with the rank of Vice-Admiral. His carriers were, fortunately, not at Pearl Harbor during the Japanese attack. He was the Commander of Task Force 16 in April 1942 during the 'Doolittle Raid', the first bombing attack on Japanese soil. By November 1942 he was C-in-C South Pacific Forces and Area, remaining in command of US Forces in that area for the next 18 months. In June 1944 he took command of the Third Fleet and was designated Commander Western Pacific Task Forces. During the Battle of Leyte Gulf his carriers were lured away from the focal point of the battle by the Japanese decoy carrier force and the US forces narrowly avoided disaster. Again his judgement was called into question when he took his ships into the teeth of two typhoons, as a result of which three destroyers were lost. Subsequent to the Okinawa campaign in 1945, his forces struck at Tokyo and the Japanese home islands. His flag was flying on USS *Missouri* in Tokyo Bay when the formal Japanese surrender was signed on board. A pugnacious man, with an impulsive nature, he was nicknamed 'Bull' Halsey, but he earned the loyalty of his commanding officer, Nimitz, when he advocated taking to the offensive as soon as possible at the beginning of the war.

HALSEY

Rank attained	Admiral
Dates	1882–1959
Background	United States Naval Academy, Annapolis
Commands	Task Force 16, 1942; C-in-C Southern Pacific, 1942; Third Fleet, 1944

Yamamoto, Nagumo and Kurita

WHO WAS WHO Japan

YAMAMOTO

Rank attained	Admiral
Dates	1884–1943
Background	Career sailor, Etajima naval academy,
Commands	C-in-C of the Combined Fleet, 1939–43

Yamamoto   Nagumo   Kurita

NAGUMO

Rank attained	Vice-Admiral
Dates	1887–1944
Background	Career sailor
Commands	C-in-C of the Combined Fleet's Carrier Strike Force, 1941–44

KURITA

Rank attained	Vice-Admiral
Dates	1889–1977
Background	Career sailor
Commands	C-in-C 7th Cruiser Squadron, 1941; Close Support Force, 1942; First Striking Force, 1944

Admiral **Isoroku Yamamoto** was responsible for the enlargement of the Japanese Navy before the war. He was wounded in action during the Russo-Japanese War of 1904–5. He later studied in the USA and was fully aware of US industrial might. He opposed the war against the USA because he thought that Japan would eventually lose, but he planned the Pearl Harbor attack as he reasoned that a pre-emptive strike was Japan's only option. Yamamoto then tried to wipe out the US carriers at the Battle of Midway but ended up being heavily defeated. On 18 April 1943 US fighters intercepted the aircraft in which he was a passenger, shot it down and killed him. Well regarded, Yamamoto was an early proponent of naval air power and understood the influence it would have on naval warfare.

Vice-Admiral **Chuichi Nagumo** was in command of the élite First Carrier Strike Force (*Kido Butai*) that attacked Pearl Harbor. Not being an aviation specialist, he was overcautious and decided not to make a third attack which could have proved deci-

sive. Again he proved to be hesitant during the Battle of Midway, paying the price by losing four aircraft carriers. He lost two more sea battles, at the Eastern Solomons and in the Santa Cruz Islands. He was then relieved of his command. Organising the defence of Saipan, when all was lost to the Americans, he committed suicide.

Vice-Admiral **Takeo Kurita** spent a large proportion of his naval career afloat. He commanded the Cruiser Squadron covering the invasion fleet that invaded Malaya and then the Dutch East Indies. He was at the battles of Midway and Leyte Gulf. At Leyte he led the First Strike Force, consisting of battleships, cruisers and destroyers. These vessels inflicted the most damage on the US ships, sinking an escort carrier and three destroyers. However, when things were getting desperate for the Americans, Kurita pulled back, his warships short of fuel.

Dowding and Harris

DOWDING

Rank attained	Air Chief Marshal
Dates	1882–1970
Background	Royal Military Academy Woolwich; Royal Flying Corps
Commands	C-in-C Fighter Command, 1940

Dowding   Harris

Hugh Dowding joined the newly created Royal Flying Corps in 1914 and fought in World War I. In 1936 he became C-in-C Fighter Command. He was resolute in his belief that the defence of Britain should not be threatened by the dispersal of precious squadrons to Norway and France during the period when their loss was inevitable, but Fighter Command was still outnumbered by four to one. Dowding clashed with other senior officers with regard to tactics, particularly the use of the 'Big Wing', the value of which he was not convinced, but in the end he was overruled. The three-month Battle of Britain ended in victory for Britain, and any hope Hitler had of launching an invasion was quashed. As many did not agree with Dowding's tactics, in November 1940 he was replaced as head of Fighter Command. He was sent to America to co-ordinate aircraft production; he retired from the Royal Air Force in July 1942. Hugh Dowding is considered to be one of the masterminds behind the victory in

the Battle of Britain – one of the crucial battles of World War II. Nicknamed 'Stuffy' because of his aloof personality, Dowding is seen as one of the most important air commanders of the war.

Arthur Harris joined the Royal Flying Corps in 1915. At the outbreak of World War II he spent the early months in the USA purchasing aircraft for Britain. He then served under Charles Portal, C-in-C of RAF Bomber Command, and became C-in-C himself in 1942. At the time, the Allied bombing campaign was ineffective and Harris set out to implement a new and more efficient strategy. Under his leadership the Command developed the technique of saturation, or area, bombing. He argued that night-time 'blanket' bombing of urban areas was the only way to defeat Germany, undermining civilian morale and destroying any factories within the cities. Attacks were launched on Germany's major population centres, sometimes involving as many as a thousand bombers. The campaign killed an estimated 600,000 civilians and destroyed or seriously damaged some 6,000,000 homes. During the war Bomber Command lost over 57,000 men killed. 'Bomber' Harris commanded great respect and loyalty from his subordinates and his bomber crews, but his request for a campaign medal for Bomber Command was refused. The morality of the bombing campaign will always be debatable.

HARRIS

Rank attained	Air Chief Marshal
Dates	1892–1984
Background	Royal Flying Corps
Commands	No 5 Bomber Group, 1939; C-in-C Bomber Command, 1942

BADER	
Rank attained	Wing Commander
Dates	1910–1982
Background	RAF fighter pilot.
Commands	No. 242 Squadron; 1940; Tangmere Wing, 1940

Bader   *Galland*

GALLAND	
Rank attained	Lt General
Dates	1912–1996
Background	Career Pilot
Commands	Gruppen III./JG 26, 1940; Geschwader JG 26, 1940; Fighter Arm, 1941; Jagdverband 44, 1945

Douglas Bader was a British fighter pilot who became a legend in his own life-time. In 1931 he lost both legs in a flying accident and was invalided out of the RAF. He was fitted with artificial legs and managing to over-come his physical disability. He was readmitted to the RAF for flying duties in 1939 and by February 1940 he was with No. 19 squadron. Fly with No. 222 Squadron he got his first kill, a Bf 109, on 1 June 1940. Later that month he was given command of No. 242 squadron, which was manned by Canadians. During the Battle of Britain he was given a Wing, three squadrons, because of his outstanding leadership qualities. He often disagreed about tactics with Fighter Command Headquarters especially with regard to the use of the 'Big Wing'. In August 1941 he collided with an enemy aircraft over Belgium and was captured. He spent the rest of the War as a POW. After escape attempts the Germans eventually sent him to the high security prison at Colditz. Before capture he shot down a total of 23 enemy aircraft.

Adolf Galland was a leading German fighter pilot and a key Luftwaffe commander. Learning to fly gliders in Germany in the early 30s he then received fighter training in Italy then joining the Luftwaffe in 1934. He volunteered for the Condor Legion in 1937, serving with Nationalist forces during the Spanish Civil War. After his service there he served in Germany as a director of ground support operations. He was serving with a ground support unit when the war began. Later he transferred to a fighter squadron for the 1940 Campaign in the West and shooting down down his first aircraft. He was then promoted to a Gruppenkommandeur and fought in the Battle of Britain, for a time he was Germany's leading ace. In 1941 he was promoted to General of the Fighter Arm at 29 years of age, the youngest general in the German services. He commanded the German fighter forces in the west for the rest of the war and was responsible for many technical innovations in aerial combat. He consistently advocated greater emphasis on the fighter arm, but was always overruled by Göring and Hitler. During the final weeks of the war he was dismissed from his post by Göring and he then organized a unit flying Me 262 jets where he was joined by a number of other German aces. He shot down seven aircraft while flying jets fighters, bringing his total to 103 aircraft.

LEMAY

Rank attained	General
Dates	1906–1990
Background	Career airman
Commands	C-inC of 305th Bombardment Group, 1942; 20th Bomber Command, 1943; 21st Bomber Command, 1945

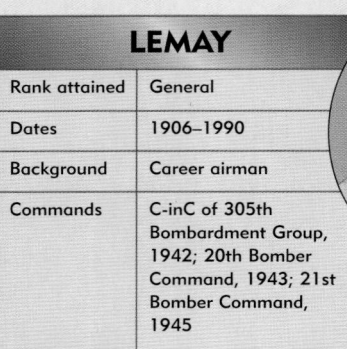

LeMay   Spaatz   Eaker

Curtis E. LeMay was one of the architects of the US bomber offensives against Germany and then Japan. A strict disciplinarian and a great tactician, he became the youngest two-star general in the US Army, commanding a bomber group. By leading raids personally, he gained the action experience to develop better defensive formations. In July 1944 he transferred to the China/Burma/India theatre to command the 20th Bomber Group. He then commanded 21st Bomber Command, greatly improving the bomber offensive against Japan. He switched to night-time, low-level, area incendiary bombing. The devastation caused to Japan's cities was on a spectacular scale.

Carl Spaatz saw action in 1916 on the Mexican border and then during World War I. He was one of the earliest of US aviators. He favoured daylight precision bombing. Firstly he commanded the US Eighth Air Force then the North African theatre, including the Twelfth Air Force, fighting in Tunisia and Sicily. When he returned to the UK he became Commanding General of the Strategic Air Force. In 1945 he transferred to the Pacific, directing the bombing of Japan.

SPAATZ

Rank attained	General
Dates	1891–1974
Background	Career airman
Commands	Eighth USAAF, 1942; C-in-C Allied Air Forces North Africa, 1943; US Stategic Air Force, Europe, 1943; US Stategic Air Force, Pacific, 1945

EAKER

Rank attained	Lieutenant-General
Dates	1896–1987
Background	Career airman
Commands	C-in-C Eighth USAAF, 1943; C-in-C Allied Air Forces Mediterranean, 1943.

Ira Eaker led the first US bombing raid on Germany in 1942. Texas-born he was an infantry officer before learning to fly and joining the United States Air Service. Promoted to Brigadier-General in 1942, Eaker was appointed C-in-C of Eighth Bomber Command under Carl Spaatz. Arriving in England in February 1942, he set up US Army Bomber Command at High Wycombe. In February 1943 he headed the US Air Force in Algiers. Eaker was a strong advocate of daylight bombing raids: the USAAF would concentrate on daylight bombing whereas the RAF would bomb at night. He was promoted to Lieutenant-General in June 1943, commanding Mediterranean Allied Air Forces.

Fighter Aces

An ace is a pilot who has managed to shoot down five or more enemy aircraft. Most fighter pilots of the various air forces did not achieve this honour.

The very high scores credited to German fighter pilots were achieved mostly on the Eastern Front, where they had a very rich target environment, particularly during the first eighteen months of the fighting – a case of quality over quantity. Against Western pilots they achieved far fewer. No limit was put on the number of combat missions or hours German pilots could fly. In the long run, this policy hampered the Luftwaffe's ability to turn out large numbers of well-trained pilots later in the war. While British and US pilots scored fewer individual kills, when they finished their tours of duty they then went on to train new pilots, giving them the full benefit of their combat experience.

Erich Hartmann, highest scoring ace

TOP SCORING ACES, BY NATION

BRITAIN AND THE DOMINIONS	
M. T. St J. 'Pat' Pattle	51
J. E. 'Johnnie' Johnson	37
W. 'Cherry' Vale	31
G. F. Beurling	31
A. G. 'Sailor' Malan	30
CZECHOSLOVAKIA	
Jan Gerthofer	33
DENMARK	
Kaj Birksted	10
FINLAND	
E. I. Juutilainen	94
FRANCE	
Marcel Albert	23
GERMANY	
Erich Hartmann	352
Gerhard Barkhorn	301
Günther Rall	275
Otto Kittel	267
Walter 'Nowi' Nowotny	258
HUNGARY	
Deszö Szentgyörgyi	34
ITALY	
Adriano Visconti	26

JAPANESE	
Tatsuzo Iwamoto	94
Hiroyoshi Nishizawa	87
Shoichi Sugita	70
Saburo Sakai	64
Takeo Okumura	54
NORWAY	
Svien Heglund	14
POLAND	
Stanislaw Skalski	21
USA	
R. I. 'Dick' Bong	40
T. B. McGuire	38
D. McCampbell	34
F. S. 'Gabby' Gabreski	28
G. 'Pappy' Boyington	28
USSR	
Ivan Kozhedub	62
Aleksandr Pokryshkin	59
Grigoriy Rechkalev	56
Nikolai Gulaev	53
Arseniy Vorozheikin	52
YUGOSLAVIA	
Cvitan Galic	36

P-38 Lightning. USAAF pilot Ira Bong scored all his 40 victories in this type

The highly-trained Japanese fighter pilots carried all before them early in the war but this very élite group was gradually whittled down. The Samurai philosophy inspired most not to carry a parachute as this implied weakness, so they paid the price. The Japanese training schools could not cope with demand and therefore standards had to be lowered.

The Soviet fighter pilots during the early years were poorly trained and badly equipped, but later the situation did improve. Altogether there were over 200 Soviet aces, some of them women. The top female ace was Lilya Litvak, who had thirteen victories to her credit.

As the war progressed, the pilot training schemes of the British and American air forces began to tell. The ever-increasing numbers of pilots they produced meant fewer opportunities for scoring individual victories over the steadily dwindling numbers of German pilots sent up to oppose them. Over Europe, most RAF pilots achieved ace status early in the war, and by 1943, with some exceptions, they jostled for aerial targets, as did their US allies. In the meantime, in the Pacific the US pilots were cutting a swathe through the Japanese. The 'Great Marianas Turkey Shoot' (Battle of the Philippine Sea) sounded the death knell of the Japanese Navy air arm, as the well-honed US Navy and Marine Corps pilots swept them from the sky. One US Navy pilot, David McCampbell, claimed seven in a single day.

Many pilots who had escaped from the countries of German-occupied Europe fought on in the air forces of the Allies or free air forces and went on to become aces.

Douglas Bader (centre), the legless RAF pilot who shot down 23 aircraft before being captured by the Germans

HIMMLER

Rank attained	Reichsführer-SS
Dates	1900–1945
Background	*Freikorps*, poultry farmer
Commands	SS, 1929; Army Group Vistula, 1945

The son of a schoolteacher, **Heinrich Himmler** trained as an officer at the end of World War I but saw no active service. He then became a poultry farmer. In 1925 he joined the Nazi party and became deputy leader of the SS in 1927 (then only 280 strong). He became its leader in January 1929. From small beginnings, under his leadership the SS expanded, and by January 1933 it numbered over 50,000. After the Nazi party came to power he organised the very efficient liquidation of the leadership of the rival SA, which then became subordinated in power to the SS. He established dominance over state security in every sphere, including the police. He established the first concentration camps. Obsessed with racial purity, he wanted the SS to be at the forefront of the Aryan ideal. He oversaw the 'Final Solution', the extermination of the Jews. He was looked upon as the natural successor to Hitler as the Führer, but when he made tentative overtures to the Allies regarding peace Hitler dismissed him from all posts and ordered his arrest. He tried to escape the Allies in disguise but was captured by the British and on May 23, 1945 he committed suicide by taking poison.

The son of a music teacher, **Reinhard Heydrich** joined the German Navy in 1922 but was forced to resign after a scandalous affair with an influential industrialist's daughter in 1931. He then joined the SS. Himmler saw his potential and promoted him to be his deputy. In 1934 he took command of the Gestapo in Berlin and eventually the Gestapo nationwide. A man noted for his total lack of mercy, he persecuted any group that he deemed as being in any way enemies of the Nazi party. With the annexation of large parts of Eastern Europe, his murder squads (*Einsatzgruppen*) were given a free hand murdering hundreds of thousands of Jews. He had a hand in drafting the 'Final Solution' and in the systematic murder of the Jews in the death camps. Shortly after being created *Reichsprotektor* of Bohemia-Moravia (occupied Czechoslovakia), on June 4, 1942, he was assassinated in Prague by a team of Free Czech agents parachuted from Britain. The village of Lidice was destroyed and the adults murdered in reprisal. Many high-ranking individuals within the Nazi party were frightened of him, being fully aware of his total lack of humanity and his very ambitious nature. Many suspected that he intended to succeed Hitler as Führer.

HEYDRICH

Rank attained	Obergruppenführer
Dates	1904–1942
Background	*Freikorps*. Cashiered from the German Navy
Commands	Deputy leader SS, 1934; Deputy Reichsprotektor of Bohemia and Moravia, 1942

Himmler   Heydrich

3 Blitzkrieg

The creator of the German tank forces, General Heinz Guderian, set out his theories on tank warfare in his book *Achtung–Panzer!* in 1937. Speed, surprise, flexibility and concentration of force were the essence of the tactic. It combined air power and fast-moving, powerful tank and mechanised infantry units which would thrust deep into enemy-held territory. These units would be supported by mobile artillery, assault engineers and dive-bombers. Strong enemy positions would be contained or bypassed, while the centre of the attack (*Schwerpunkt*) was directed at the weakest point of the enemy's defences. Good radio communications were vital to the fast-moving assaults. The enemy positions that had been bypassed or contained would be dealt with by slower-moving follow-up formations. The opposing forces would continue to be outpaced and enveloped as attacks would continue after the break-through, generating disorder and terror among the enemy troops. Airborne troops could also be utilised by landing on vital centres in the rear of the front, holding them until relieved by more conventional units.

The *Blitzkrieg* ('lightning war') was first used during the Polish campaign in September 1939. After the success of this and the Scandinavia campaigns, it was used much more dramatically in the conquest of Belgium, the Netherlands and France, where the concept worked better than anyone could expect. In early 1941 came the taking of Yugoslavia and Greece. Initially the advance into Russia went well, but with very long lines of communication it was found that the Germans were unable to maintain the necessary momentum. The tactic would later be used by the Soviet forces against the Germans.

A brilliant advocate of the *Blitzkrieg* was General Erwin Rommel. He had commanded the 7th Panzer Division with stunning success during the Battle for France in 1940. Then he took command of the *Afrika Korps* in the spring of 1941, and came very close to defeating the British 8th Army even though he was always outnumbered. Eventually he was stopped by much larger and better equipped Allied forces after nearly two years of combat in North Africa.

A German Mk III tank and supporting infantry during the early Blitzkrieg era

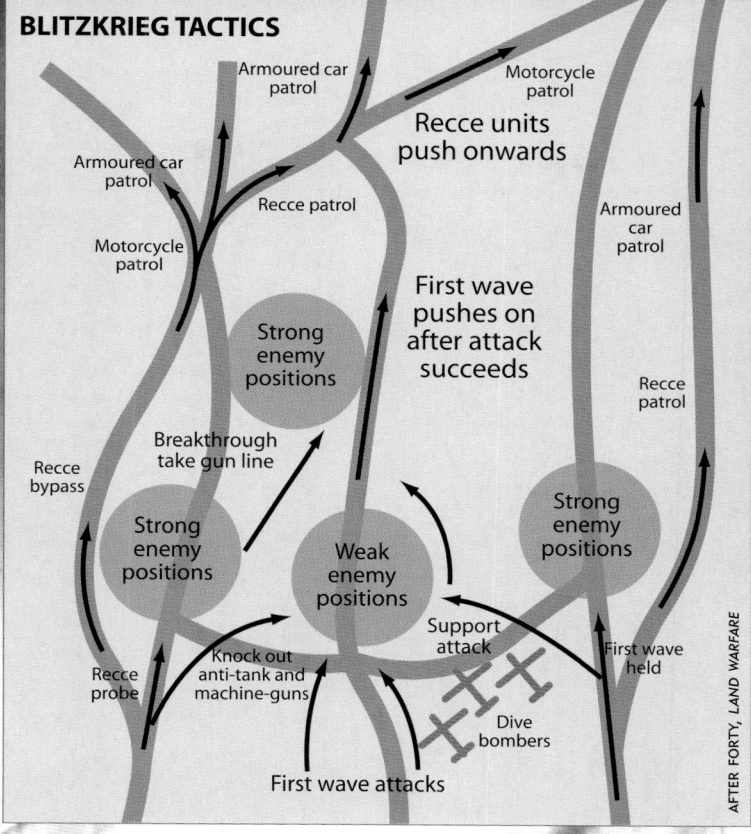

BLITZKRIEG TACTICS

Armoured car
patrol

Motorcycle
patrol

Recce units
push onwards

Armoured car
patrol

Recce patrol

Armoured
car
patrol

Motorcycle
patrol

First wave
pushes on
after attack
succeeds

Strong
enemy
positions

Recce
patrol

Recce
bypass

Breakthrough
take gun line

Strong
enemy
positions

Weak
enemy
positions

Strong
enemy
positions

Support
attack

Recce
probe

Knock out
anti-tank and
machine-guns

First wave
held

Dive
bombers

First wave attacks

AFTER FORTY, *LAND WARFARE*

Panzers advance at the
Battle of Kursk, 1943

3 Artillery

WAR TECHNOLOGY

During World War II artillery needed to be very mobile, in contrast to the demands of the previous conflict, which had generally been characterised by static trench warfare. As the war progressed, an increasing number of guns of all calibres were mounted on tracked vehicles as, for example, self-propelled guns and tank destroyers. Some German guns remained horse-drawn throughout the war.

The most numerous type of artillery were field guns and howitzers, e.g., the 105mm guns of Germany and the USA and the British 25pdr. Next most numerous were heavy guns such as the 155mm and 8in calibre weapons. Free-flight rockets were used *en masse*, particularly by the Russian Army.

The Germans soon realised that their 88mm anti-aircraft gun was easily adaptable for use against tanks – its high-velocity shells could pierce Allied armour at very long range.

Anti-aircraft artillery saw the first use of proximity-fused shells, which with the aid of shell-mounted sensors, would explode near the target, thus causing lethal damage even without making a direct hit.

USA 155mm 'Long Tom' SP Gun	
Weight	58,000lb
Length	12ft 3in
Range	25,000yds
Shell weight	95lb
Muzzle velocity	2,800ft/sec
Calibre	6in

US 155mm 'Long Tom' self-propelled gun

British 25pdr Field Gun	
Weight	3,960lb
Length	8ft 11in
Range	13,400yds
Shell weight	25lb
Muzzle velocity	2,000ft/sec
Calibre	3.45in

British 25pdr field gun

German 88mm Flak 18	
Weight	4,985lb
Length	16ft 2in
Range	16,000yds
Shell weight	21lb
Muzzle velocity	2,690ft/sec
Calibre	3.46in

German 88mm gun and the half-track for towing it

Small Arms 3

WAR TECHNOLOGY

Small arms had not changed a great deal from those used in World War I but in the second war a greater use was made of light machine-guns and submachine-guns. As the war progressed, new semi-automatic rifles such as the American M1 Garand, the German Gew 43 and the Soviet Tokarev SVT38 made their mark. The German MG34 and 42 saw the advent of the general purpose machine-gun, which could be configured for use in the light as well as the medium role.

Lee-Enfield No 4

British Bren Light Machine-gun

Weight	22lb 5oz
Length	45.25in
Capacity	30-round magazine
Rate of fire	500 rpm
Muzzle velocity	2,400ft/sec
Calibre	.303in

British Lee-Enfield No 4 Rifle

Weight	9lb 1oz
Length	44.5in
Capacity	10-round magazine
Rate of fire	Single-shot, bolt action
Muzzle velocity	2,400ft/sec
Calibre	.303in

Bren light machine-gun

MP40 Submachine-gun

US 1919A4 Machine-gun

Weight	31lb 0oz
Length	41in
Capacity	250-round belt
Rate of fire	500 rpm
Muzzle velocity	2,800ft/sec
Calibre	.30in

German MP40 Submachine-gun

Weight	8lb 12oz
Length	32.75in
Capacity	32-round magazine
Rate of fire	500 rpm
Muzzle velocity	1,250ft/sec
Calibre	9mm

1919A4 Medium machine-gun

3 Bombing

A Liberator heavy bomber

The USAAF remained convinced that daylight bombing would achieve the best results by using aircraft with a very heavy defensive armament that could fight their way through to the target. Even so, they would suffer heavy casualties. Early in the war the RAF had suffered high casualties in daylight raids, and they switched to night bombing in an attempt to reduce them.

Level bombing during the first years of the war was a very impre-

Blenheim light bomber

cise art, especially at night. Collateral damage was always high. Aircraft would rain down hundreds of bombs in order to get a few hits on a target such as a factory, and often they would completely miss it. Navigation at night was almost impossible. The Luftwaffe were the first to use radio beams to aid their aircraft during their nocturnal *Blitz* on Great

Britain during 1940–41. The RAF at the time were lucky even to find the target at night, and daylight raids had proved to be far too costly in terms of casualties. Things improved for the British in 1942 with the 'Gee' navigational aid, providing navigators with a fix from radio pulses transmitted by three ground stations, the pulses intersecting at the target.

Area-bombing of urban centres was adopted when precision bombing could not be achieved, the target being an entire city with its factories and people. It was hoped that this would undermine the morale of the civilian population. It worked in a few places. The Netherlands surrendered after Rotterdam's town centre had been flattened by German bombers, but area-bombing did not undermine the will of Britons, Germans or Japanese to continue to fight the war.

Dornier Do17 bomber

The firestorm was achieved by using a combination of high explosive and incendiaries. The high-explosive bombs would be dropped to break up buildings, making them more susceptible to the incendiaries. Huge numbers of small incendiary bombs would be dropped over a whole city. When areas caught fire, the air above would become hot and rise rapidly. At ground level cold air would then rush in, feeding the fire with oxygen and making it burn ever more vigorously. As the fires joined up, wind speeds in excess of 150mph could be generated, which would in turn continue to fuel the fires. The most notable examples of this tactic occurred in Hamburg in 1943, Dresden in 1945 and Tokyo in 1945: 40,000 people were killed in Hamburg, as many as 150,000 in Dresden and 100,000 in Tokyo.

Dive-bombing made it possible for pin-point accuracy to be achieved. Targets such as bridges and ships could be taken out with amazing accuracy. A typical Stuka attack would commence from about 10,000 feet in an 80-degree dive, the drag of the aircraft's fixed undercarriage and the dive brakes preventing the speed from increasing too rapidly. This made for a stable aircraft during the 15-second dive. The pilot centred the bombsight on the target, released his bomb-load at 2,200 feet, then automatically pulled out of the dive.

Swordfish torpedo-bomber

Another successful dive-bomber was the US Navy's Douglas Dauntless. This aircraft sank four Japanese aircraft carriers at the decisive Battle of Midway. As the war progressed, the slow dive-bomber was always vulnerable to fighters and it was eventually supplanted by the fighter-bomber.

Torpedo-bombers brought many mighty warships to bay, for instance the battleships at Taranto and Pearl Harbor, and also crippled the *Bismarck* before her destruction by British battleships. Torpedo-bombers would attack from an altitude of 100 feet or less and might split up, approaching from different directions. At 1,000 yards from the target the torpedo would be released. A 45-knot torpedo launched at 1,000 yards takes 40 seconds to reach a ship. In that time the ship would travel 2,000 feet if moving at 30 knots. Aim was important: the torpedo had to hit the water flat to run true to the target or else it might dive straight down or porpoise. The torpedo was designed to run at a pre-set depth just below the surface.

V-Weapons

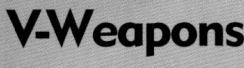

V-1 flying bomb

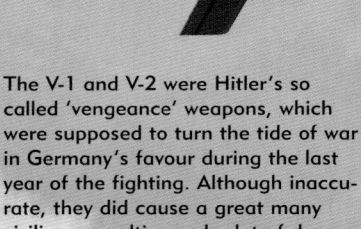

The V-1 and V-2 were Hitler's so called 'vengeance' weapons, which were supposed to turn the tide of war in Germany's favour during the last year of the fighting. Although inaccurate, they did cause a great many civilian casualties and a lot of damage, but they failed in their purpose.

The V-1 was nicknamed the 'Doodlebug' by the British and the 'Buzz Bomb' by the US. The first fell on London on June 13, 1944, and by the end of the war they had caused over 6,000 British deaths and nearly 18,000 injured. Of the 10,000 or more launched against London, however, only 3,500 got through, the rest falling short or being shot down.

From October 1944 Belgian cities came under heavy attack from V-1s, the main targets being Antwerp and Liège. Over 6,500 were fired at Antwerp, 4,000 of which landed, and over 3,000 against Liège.

V-1 Flying Bomb	
Guidance	Preset compass and auto pilot
Weight	4,800lb
Warhead	1,875lb
Range	125–250 miles
Engine	Argus pulse-jet engine, max speed 350mph
Dimensions	Length: 27ft 3in Wing Span: 17ft 4in
Production	Over 30,000

The majority of V-1s were launched from inclined ramps in France, and Holland, but some were air-launched from Heinkel 111 bombers.

More than 1,100 V-2 rockets were launched from the Netherlands against London: half of these fell short, the other half killing nearly 2,750 people and injuring 6,500 more. Antwerp received 1,350 V-2 rocket attacks, Liège 98 and Brussels 65. These combined V-1 and V-2 attacks killed nearly 3,500 Belgian civilians and almost 700 Allied servicemen.

V-2 rocket

V-2 Rocket	
Guidance	Preset, gyroscopic
Weight	28,650lb
Warhead	2,150lb
Range	200 miles
Engine	Liquid-fuelled rocket motor, max speed 3,500mph
Dimensions	Length: 46ft 1in Fin span: 11ft 8in
Production	10,000

The Atomic Bomb

In 1939 scientists in America had become convinced that Germany was developing a nuclear weapon. When the US entered the war she co-operated with Britain and the two countries began to develop their own weapon, codenamed the 'Manhattan Project'. An international team of very prominent physicists, many being émigrés from Fascist Europe, was set up under the direction of J. Robert Oppenheimer and based at Los Alamos in New Mexico.

In the meantime, a plant in occupied Norway that was producing heavy water for the Germans was destroyed by British Special Forces and Norwegian resistance fighters in November 1942. This heavy water was necessary in the production process of a nuclear weapon. The raid set the German nuclear programme back by an estimated two years. In 1944 Germany's chances of producing a bomb were finally ended by Norwegian agents, who sank the ferry containing all the remaining heavy water stocks.

Three bombs were completed at Los Alamos, the first being successfully tested on July 16, 1945. The second, called 'Little Boy', was dropped on Hiroshima on August 6, 1945 after the Japanese rejected a call for surrender. It exploded with the force of nearly 13,000 tons of TNT. Over 80,000 people were killed and 4.2 square miles of the city flattened. Still Japan refused to surrender, so a second bomb, 'Fat Man', was dropped on Nagasaki three days later, killing over 35,000. Not until August 15 did the Japanese surrender.

 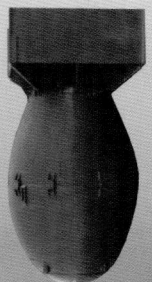

'Little Boy'   'Fat Man'

3 Amphibious Warfare

Between 1939 and 1942 amphibious techniques were poor. The Japanese Army was probably the best during this period, developing the necessary expertise as well as specialised landing craft. The Germans carried out a well-organised amphibious invasion of Norway in 1940, but they were not fully geared for an assault on Great Britain and the German Army balked at the idea.

The most vulnerable and important moment of an amphibious landing is when the first wave of troops hits the beach and the complex timing of the sea bombardment and air support comes fully into play.

During the disastrous raid on the French port of Dieppe by the British and Canadians in August 1942, some very serious lessons had to be learnt – a very thorough surveying of the beach beforehand, a heavy naval and air bombardment prior to disembarkation, support vessels covering the beach as the troops land, the need to develop specialised equipment, landing ships and landing craft, and the efficient co-ordination of landing supplies on the beach. Many of these lessons had not been fully absorbed in time for the

Allied landings in North Africa three months later. Needless numbers of troops were drowned, each man being overburdened with gear and there being nothing adequately to bridge the gap between the shore and the landing vessels. Thankfully the landings were largely unopposed. These

British tanks and vehicles disembark from a large landing ship

lessons were learnt for the subsequent landings on Sicily and Italy and also for the D-Day landings, the largest and most complex amphibious operation the world has ever seen.

The US Marines were the masters of amphibious operational techniques. As in most things, experience counts, and the US Marines certainly got plenty of that as they made their spectacular island-hopping offensive across the Pacific Ocean.

US Marines hit the beach

Airborne Forces

Airborne troops can be landed by parachute, by large troop-carrying gliders or by conventional transport aircraft.

The Soviets were the first to form airborne units in the 1930s, but they made little use of them during the war.

The German Luftwaffe formed their first airborne troops in 1938 and they were the first to use them operationally during the invasion of the West in 1940, most notably in the taking of the powerful fort of Eben Emael in Belgium. The largest German air landing was against Crete in 1941. Even though successful, 4,000 men were lost out of 15,000 involved.

British and US airborne units made airborne assaults during the invasion of Sicily in 1943. During the successful D-Day invasion three airborne divisions were landed by parachute and glider, the US 82nd and 101st divisions, and the British 6th Division. Three months later, during operation 'Market Garden', Allied airborne troops were to take important bridges in Holland. The courageous attempts to capture the bridge at Arnhem ended in a failure for the British and Polish troops involved.

The Allied crossing of the Rhine in March 1945 was the largest air landing carried out on a single day – 22,000 troops.

Airborne forces were employed during the Pacific and Far Eastern campaigns but never to the extent that they were in Europe.

Airborne troops were always highly motivated and particularly well trained, but airborne operations always generated high casualty rates. This is due to the nature of airborne operations, the troops being relatively lightly equipped and generally employed upon highly risky undertakings. When fighting enemy units with tanks and heavy artillery, as at Arnhem, they find themselves at a huge disadvantage. After the battle for Crete, Hitler decided that large-scale airborne operations were too costly, and from then on German airborne troops were used as conventional infantry, albeit with considerable success.

A German paratrooper

British Horsa glider, capable of transporting 25 troops a light artillery piece or a Jeep

3 Jungle Warfare

WAR TECHNOLOGY

The jungle is an extremely challenging environment in which to survive, let alone fight. To soldiers from Europe and America it was a strange, fearsome place, and moving and fighting in it a nightmare. Many were ready to classify the jungle as impenetrable, since it appeared only as an obstacle to movement, not an asset. Because of this attitude, the British paid the penalty during the campaign for Malaya in 1941. The Japanese were also unused to jungle – many of their soldiers were from temperate environments – but they realised that it created a good environment making for concealment and for outflanking manoeuvres.

Careful training in survival skills was essential, and these had to be learnt by Western soldiers. Maintaining good health and hygiene to avoid sickness, and learning the skills of navigating the jungle where it was impossible to see much further than ten yards ahead, enabled the troops to survive as well as fight. Essential skills such as tracking, jungle patrolling, clearing villages, watching for booby traps and ambush had to be learnt. Learning how to get within ten yards of the enemy without being seen was also vital. Troops had to

acclimatise to cope with the heat and humidity, and also the torrential rain, the mud, the insects and animals and the potential for sickness, especially malaria and dysentery in the hot and sticky conditions. Sickness often caused more casualties than the enemy.

The close-quarters fighting often encountered in the jungle demanded special equipment such as carbines, automatic weapons and machetes. The proper use of camouflage helped to make up for an enemy with superior numbers.

Units such as the Chindits, who operated deep behind enemy lines in northern Burma, became experts in jungle combat. For many months they lived in, and fought the enemy in, the jungles of Japanese-held territory, totally reliant on airdrops for their supplies. The environment led to the loss of many men, both in combat and to sickness.

The US Marines and soldiers operating in the tropics of the Pacific Ocean also became masters of the art of jungle combat as they pushed the Japanese back.

GIs in a typical jungle environment in New Guinea

Electronic Warfare

An Enigma machine

One of the most important developments of the war was **radar** (radio detection and ranging) which uses radio waves to detect the presence of distant objects. From 1934 it had been developed by most of the world's powers and was immediately seen as a way of detecting aircraft and providing early warning of an air attack. It proved particularly useful during the Battle of Britain in 1940, the British having established, pre-war, a chain of radar stations known as 'Chain Home', and indeed was critical in winning that battle for the British. As the war progressed it was increasingly fitted to ships and aircraft, proving very important during the Battle of the Atlantic. During the bombing campaign counter-measures had to be taken by the Allies in order to disrupt and confuse the German radars. One method was to drop large amounts of thin strips of tin foil ('window') which reflected the radar beams, saturating the German radar stations with huge numbers of false targets.

Radio navigation systems were used by both sides to assist bombers in locating targets. An early German system named 'Knickebein' utilised two transmitting stations: the bomber crews flew along the steady 'note lane' from the first radio transmitter, releasing their bombs when they passed through the steady 'note lane' from a second transmitter as it crossed the first. The British used similar systems employing ground stations such as Gee-H and 'Oboe', and the US 'Shoran'.

The **Enigma cipher machine** was used by the Germans to encode their military signals, each German military unit needing a machine to encipher and decipher coded messages. It was an electro-mechanical device relying on a series of rotating wheels to scramble messages into incoherent ciphertext. Both the transmitting and receiving Enigmas were set to the same code: if you knew how the rotors were set you got the message, if not just a stream of indecipherable and random letters. The machine could be set to many millions of combinations, each one generating a completely different ciphertext message. In 1940 British code breakers stationed at Bletchley Park managed to crack the Enigma code resulting in the 'Ultra' codebreakers. By the summer of 1944 they were using the world's first electronic computer to speed the process.

A German Ju 88 night-fighter showing the radar antennae on its nose

German Army

The Field Army was organised into army groups, then armies and army corps. In 1944 there were 11 army groups controlling 26 armies with the division being the basic unit. In 1939 a division was approximately 17,500 strong although by 1944 the established strength had been reduced to just over 12,500. 304 divisions had been formed, of which 31 had been Panzer divisions. During the war the German Army mobilised 12½ million men; over three million of these were killed and seven million wounded.

In September 1939 Germany invaded Poland with 60 out of a total of 106 divisions – nearly 1½ million men. When invading the West in 1940, the Army deployed 2½ million men with 2,500 tanks in 135 divisions. Three million men were deployed in June 1941 for the invasion of Russia, comprising 160 divisions and nearly 4,000 tanks. After June 1941 never less than 60% of the German Army's strength was deployed on the Russian Front.

Employing revolutionary *Blitzkrieg* tactics, the German Army cut a swathe across Europe and within the first twelve months of hostilities had the greater part of western Europe under its control. 1941 then saw the conquest of the Balkans as well as General Rommel's Afrika Korps slicing through the British Army in North Africa.

The June 1941 invasion of Russia opened with a whole series of

German infantryman

German troops in Russia

Jagdpanther tank destroyer

German victories until halted by the atrocious weather of the Russian winter. The Army had not been equipped with the appropriate winter gear, having anticipated that the Russian Army would be beaten before the winter arrived. In 1942, with the return of warmer weather, the successes continued until halted by the battle for Stalingrad during the winter of 1942/43. After the German defeat at the Battle of Kursk, in the summer of 1943, Soviet forces always held the initiative.

On June 6, 1944 – D-Day – the Allied forces from England landed in Normandy. The German Army deployed 58 divisions in the West, ten being Panzer divisions, to counter this. They were now having to contend with a war being fought on two fronts. There were some counter-offensives – such as that at the Battle of the Bulge, but the eventual outcome was inevitable.

The German soldier was very professional and well trained, aggressive in attack and stubborn in defence.

He was always adaptable, particularly in the later years of the war, when shortages of equipment were being felt.

Even though not part of the regular Army, Waffen-SS divisions fought alongside it. By May 1945, 38 divisions had been recruited, having enlisted 800,000 men, although, of these, only a half a dozen were fully fledged combat units. These divisions often received the best equipment, especially tanks. Used as a type of combat 'fire brigade', they were often able to stabilise a battlefield crisis. The Waffen-SS played a critical role on all the fronts, apart from that in North Africa. They achieved a considerable reputation for their endurance in battle and were looked upon as an élite force. This reputation was only matched by that for cruelty, and many war crimes and atrocities were committed. Some units were recruited from the peoples of conquered countries. Altogether nearly one in four of their number would die in battle.

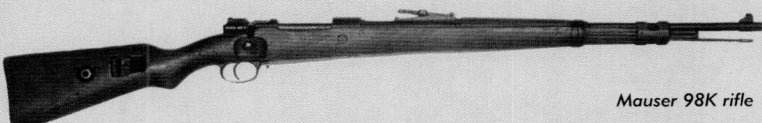

Mauser 98K rifle

Panzers

Determined not to repeat the stale-mate of the trenches of World War I, the German Army made tanks a high priority. The first *Panzer* (armoured) division was formed in 1935, and these units operated independently of more conventional formations. *Panzer* divisions spearheaded the *Blitzkrieg* concept of fast, mobile, offensive warfare that dominated the first half of the war.

The first *Panzer* was the PzKpfw I of 1934, armed only with machine-guns and weighing just 5 tons. By the end of the war the Germans were operating the heaviest tanks of the war, Tiger IIs of 70 tons armed with one of the most powerful tank guns of the war, the 88mm L/71.

In addition to the various marks of tanks built (PzKpfw I, II, 35/38(t), III, IV, V and VI), there were numerous armoured assault guns and tank destroyers. Built on the same hulls as the tanks, but easier to construct, these turretless combat vehicles proved particularly useful in the defensive role that the German Army was forced to adopt during the later years of the war.

PzKpfw IV

Weight	25 tons
Crew	Five
Armament	One 75mm gun and two 7.92mm MG 34 machine-guns
Armour	Max: 80mm. Min: 10mm
Engine	Maybach, 300hp, speed 26mph
Dimensions	Length: 19ft 5in. Width: 9ft 7in. Height: 8ft 6in
Production	8,500

PzKpfw IV

PzKpfw VI Tiger

PzKpfw V PANTHER

Weight	44.8 tons
Crew	Five
Armament	One 75mm gun and two 7.92mm MG 34 machine-guns
Armour	Max: 120mm. Min: 15mm
Engine	Maybach, 690hp, speed 34mph
Dimensions	Length: 29ft 1in. Width: 10ft 10in. Height: 9ft 8in
Production	5,500

PzKpfw VI TIGER I

Weight	54.1 tons
Crew	Five
Armament	One 88mm gun and two 7.92mm MG 34 machine-guns
Armour	Max. 120mm Min: 26mm
Engine	Maybach, 694hp, speed 23mph
Dimensions	Length: 27ft 9in. Width: 12ft 3in. Height: 9ft 6in
Production	1,354

PzKpfw V Panther

PzKpfw 38(t)

In December 1939 the 'pocket battle-ship' *Admiral Graf Spee* was scuttled after the famous Battle of the River Plate action with British cruisers. Along with her two sister ships, *Lützow* (ex *Deutschland*) and *Admiral Scheer*, she made up a revolutionary class of small battleships. Ideal for long-range commerce raiding, they sank or captured some 30 Allied merchant ships.

The *Scharnhorst* and *Gneisenau* were superbly equipped battle-cruisers. They were fast, well armed and well armoured. Between them they sank a British aircraft carrier, two destroyers, an armed merchant cruiser and 22 Allied merchant ships.

The *Scharnhorst* was eventually brought to bay and sunk by Royal Navy warships at the Battle of the North Cape in December 1943.

The mighty sisters *Bismarck* and *Tirpitz* were the most formidable German battle-ships of World War II. After the *Bismarck* had sunk HMS *Hood*, the pride of the British Fleet, she was hunted down and then pounded into submission by British battleships'

guns and sunk in the Atlantic in May 1941. *Tirpitz* was targeted and sunk by RAF Lancaster bombers using 5.5-ton 'Tallboy' high-penetration bombs.

Deutschland Class	
Displacement	15,000 tons
Crew	950
Armament	6 x 11in, 8 x 5.9in guns
Armour	Max: 152mm. Min: 45mm
Engine/motor	8 MAN diesels, 44,000hp, max. speed 26 knots
Dimensions	Length: 610ft 3in Beam 70ft 0in

Pocket Battleship
Graf Spee

Battlecruiser
Gneisenau

Scharnhorst Class	
Displacement	38,000 tons
Crew	1,700
Armament	9 x 11in & 12 x 5.9in guns
Armour	Max: 350mm. Min: 35mm
Engine/motor	Twelve turbines, 160,000hp, max. speed 32 knots
Dimensions	Length: 753ft 11in Beam 98ft 5in

Bismarck Class	
Displacement	51,000 tons
Crew	2,092
Armament	8 x 15in & 12 x 5.9in guns
Armour	Max: 360mm. Min: 35mm
Engine/motor	Twelve turbines, 163,000hp, max. speed 30 knots
Dimensions	Length: 813ft 8in Beam 118ft 1in

Battleship Bismarck

U-Boats

1,170 U-boats were built during the war, of which 1,000 went on operations. Of these 781 were lost – a loss rate of nearly 80%.

The workhorse of the German submarine fleet was the Type VII. A good design, it underwent many updates and improvements, the main model being the Type VIIC.

U-boats only dived when necessary: they were designed for a good surface speed and a long range on diesel engines. While they were submerged they could only operate on battery-powered electric motors, and these had a very limited endurance – one hour at 9 knots or four days at 2 knots, though after one day the air would become fouled. They tended to make attacks at night, on the surface, using their high speed and low silhouette in order to avoid detection.

In the latter part of the war schnorkels began to be fitted, giving the U-boats the means to run their

powerful diesel engines while submerged, as these needed oxygen to operate.

The new Type XXI boats began to enter service as the war was drawing to a close. They had a greatly increased battery capacity and a much better top speed when operating on either diesel engines or electric motors.

Type VIIC	
Displacement	865 tons
Crew	44
Armament	4 x 21in torpedo tubes forward, one aft. 1 x 88mm gun and 1 x 20mm AA gun
Range	8,500 miles surfaced
Engine/motor	3,200hp surfaced, 750hp submerged, max. speed: surfaced 17.5 knots, submerged 7 knots
Dimensions	Length: 218ft 3in Beam 20ft 3in
Production	705

Type VIIC

Type IXC	
Displacement	1,250 tons
Crew	49
Armament	4 x 21in torpedo tubes forward, 2 aft. 1 x 105mm gun, 1 x 37mm AA and 1 x 20mm AA gun
Range	13,500 miles surfaced
Engine/motor	4,400hp surfaced, 1,000hp submerged, max. speed: surfaced 18.2 knots, submerged 7.7 knots
Dimensions	Length: 252ft 3in Beam 22ft 9in
Production	163

Type XXI	
Displacement	1,650 tons
Crew	57
Armament	6 x 21in torpedo tubes forward, 4 x 30mm AA guns or 4 x 20mm AA guns
Range	15,500 miles surfaced
Engine/motor	4,800hp surfaced, 226hp submerged, max. speed: surfaced 17.5 knots, submerged 16 knots
Dimensions	Length: 251ft 9in Beam 21ft 9in
Production	118 (1,300 planned)

Type VIIC

The Luftwaffe 4

Bf 109 fighter

109, the formidable Focke-Wulf 190 fighter, and the multi-role Ju 88 were equal to the best the Allies had to offer. Indeed, German aviation technologists were developing more advanced aircraft, including the Me

Messerschmitt Bf 109E-1	
Weight	5,875lb (fully loaded)
Crew	One
Armament	Two 20mm cannon and two 7.92mm machine-guns
Range	400 miles
Engine	Daimler-Benz, 1,100hp, max. speed 354mph
Dimensions	Length: 28ft 4in Wing span: 32ft 4in Height: 8ft 2in
Production	30,500 (all marks)

Initially the Luftwaffe operated purely in a tactical capacity as the Wehrmacht swept all before it. The first setback was defeat during Battle of Britain in the summer of 1940. But its tactics continued to be successful in the skies over the Balkans, North Africa and Russia until 1942/1943, when the Allies slowly began to wrest air superiority.

The main failing of the German Air Force was that it did not have the correct aircraft – i.e., heavy bombers – to operate successfully at the strategic level as did the RAF's Bomber Command and the US 8th Air Force.

Even so, such aircraft as the Bf

262, the world's first operational jet combat plane, which could have turned the tide in the Luftwaffe's favour had it entered the fray earlier. As it was, much research and development was wasted on often futuristic projects that would have appeared too late to make a difference.

Junkers Ju 87D-1 Stuka	
Weight	5,875lb (fully loaded)
Crew	Two
Armament	Three 7.92mm machine-guns, 3,968lb max. bomb-load
Range	950 miles
Engine	Junkers Jumo, 1,400hp, max. speed 255mph
Dimensions	Length: 37ft 8in Wing span: 45ft 3in Height: 12ft 9in
Production	9,700 (all marks)

Heinkel He 111H-16	
Weight	5,875lb (fully loaded)
Crew	Five
Armament	One 20mm cannon and 4 or 5 7.92mm machine-guns, 7,000lb max. bomb-load
Range	1,200 miles
Engine	Two Junkers Jumo, 1,350hp, max. speed 252mph
Dimensions	Length: 53ft 9in Wing span: 74ft 1in Height: 13ft 1in
Production	7,300 (all marks)

Ju 87D Stuka dive-bomber

He 111 bomber

Germany's Allies

Romania had two of its provinces, Bessarabia and Northern Bukovina, forcibly annexed by the Soviet Union in June 1940, but the Romanians' obsolete army could do nothing about this so they began to reorganise and modernise with the aid of 18,000 German military advisors. This modernisation was not completed when the Germans invaded the USSR in June 1941. Even so, and always poorly equipped, the Romanians joined with the Germans, retaking their lost provinces and advancing east. They became heavily involved in the Battle of Stalingrad, where their casualties were enormous. In August 1944 there was a *coup* in Romania and the new government changed sides and joined the Allies against Germany. During the war casualties were in the region of 350,000 soldiers killed.

Hungary began acquiring territory from its neighbours in October 1939, firstly from Slovakia and then, in 1940, from Romania. Allied with Germany, she participated in the invasion of Yugoslavia, occupying one of its regions. Hungary's generally poorly equipped army again joined with the Germans and declared war on Russia

in 1941. As the war progressed the Hungarian forces were gradually to become less involved in the fighting. Eventually the Soviets occupied Budapest on October 15, 1944, after a cease-fire had been agreed. Estimates of casualties vary, but possibly as many as 150,000 died.

Bulgaria was officially at war only with Great Britain and then the USA. Following the Balkans campaign in 1941, Bulgaria occupied parts of Greece. She also aided the Germans during their occupation of parts of Yugoslavia. As the Soviet Army began to approach the Bulgarian frontier there was a military *coup* and Bulgaria made peace with the Allies and changed sides. During the last nine months of the war the Bulgarians lost over 6,500 soldiers killed and nearly 22,000 wounded while fighting the Germans.

With the fall of France, the Germans allowed a collaborationist French State to exist in the southern provinces of the country, with its capital at Vichy, headed by Marshal Pétain. Vichy French forces fought against the Allies in French North Africa, French West Africa, Madagascar and Syria.

Hungarian troops with their German-pattern helmets

The origins of the SS (*Schutzstaffeln*, or Protection Squad), or 'Black Shirts', date back to 1923 when Hitler formed the *Stabswache* (Head-quarters Guard), his personal body-guard. From small beginnings it expanded rapidly when Himmler was appointed as its head in 1929.

Himmler wanted to create a state security force that was made up of a racial élite, to be in the vanguard of National Socialism. Until 1934 it was in the shadow of the much larger, and rival, SA (*Sturmabtielungen*–Storm Troopers) under the leadership of Ernst Röhm. During the 'Night of the Long Knives', in June 1934, the SS assassinated all the members of the SA leadership, thus supplanting it as the dominant organisation within the Nazi party.

Himmler then incorporated the German police forces into the SS, thus assuming total control of the German domestic security force which in 1939 was nearly 250,000 strong.

The SS was a complex political, commercial and military organisation made up of three separate and dis-tinct branches. The Allgemeine-SS (General SS) was the main branch, serving in a political and administra-tive role. The SS-*Totenkopfverband* (SS Death's Head Organisation) and, later, the Waffen-SS (Armed SS), were the other two branches that made up the structure of the SS.

The Gestapo (*Geheime Staats-polizei*–Secret State Police) was formed by Hermann Göring in 1933. In 1939 it came under the control of Reinhard Heydrich, Himmler's subor-dinate in the SS. Even though it retained its individual identity, the Gestapo was, in effect, merged with the SS. The confinement of suspects without trial was normal, and the use of torture during interrogation was commonplace.

The Waffen-SS were independent combat units of the SS, not being part of the Army or the police. By 1939 their strength was 18,000. By June 1941 this had grown to 150,000 and by the end of 1944 it had reached 600,000. The Waffen-SS operated under the tactical control of the German Army but enjoyed prefer-ential treatment with regard to mili-tary equipment. Well known for its toughness in battle, the SS had a tendency not to take prisoners. Their members were looked upon as an élite force.

At the start of hostilities the Italian Army had 72 divisions, mostly unmechanised infantry. The majority were poorly trained and poorly equipped. There were only three armoured divisions and these also were badly equipped. A great many Italian tanks were of the two-man tankette variety and were no match for the British armour.

Italian M11/39 tanks

Italy entered the war in June 1940, invaded France, which was on the verge of collapse, and declared war on Britain.

The Italian leader, Benito Mussolini, had a large Italian Army based in Libya, of several hundred thousand troops. In neighbouring Egypt the British Army had but 36,000 men guarding the Suez Canal. On September 13, 1940, Marshal Graziani, with five Italian divisions,

Italian troops

advanced into Egypt but stopped in front of the main British defences at Mersa Matruh. The British mounted a counter-offensive on December 9, 1940 and inflicted heavy casualties on the Italians, who were thrown out of Egypt and back more than 300 miles into Libya. It was only with the aid of the German Afrika Korps that the Italian Army avoided losing Libya.

In the meantime, in October 1940, Mussolini also declared war on the Greeks, but the Italian Army's attempts to invade Greece ended in total failure.

The Italian Army also sent many thousands of men to fight in the Russian campaign in support of Germany.

When Allied forces invaded Sicily and then Italy in the summer of 1943, there were only some 12 divisions available for home defence. They were soon defeated.

Italian troops, North Africa, late 1940

The handsome and well-designed ships of the Italian Navy joined the war in June 1940. It had six battleships, two of them very modern ships (later joined by two more), 22 cruisers, 59 large fleet destroyers and 67 small escort destroyers, and 113 submarines. This fleet outnumbered the British Mediterranean Fleet, but it was handicapped by a lack of technical expertise with radar and asdic (sonar), plus the absence of any aircraft carriers.

The four modern battleships of the *Vittorio Veneto* class compared well with foreign designs. One of them was among the three battleships disabled during the attack on Taranto harbour by Royal Navy Swordfish torpedo bombers during November 1940. Another was sunk by German bombers using radio-guided bombs, after Italy surrendered to the Allies.

Italy lost twelve of its cruisers. The largest single loss was at the Battle of Matapan in March 1941 when three of the four heavy *Zara* Class ships (plus two destroyers) were sunk by British warships.

Italy's fleet destroyers were large, well-armed ships and the smaller

escort destroyers of the anti-submarine arm were acknowledged as being very efficient. Nevertheless the total losses were high: 70% of the destroyers that entered service were sunk.

Navigatori Class Destroyers	
Displacement	2,600 tons
Crew	224
Armament	6 x 4.7in guns & 4 x 21in torpedo tubes
Engine/motor	Two turbines, 50,000hp, max. speed 38 knots
Dimensions	Length: 352ft 0in Beam 33ft 5in

Navigatori *destroyer*
Da Noli

Zara *Class
cruiser* Fiume

Vittorio Veneto Class Battleships	
Displacement	45,000 tons
Crew	1,900
Armament	9 x 15in, 12 x 6in guns
Armour	Max: 350mm. Min: 60mm
Engine	Eight turbines, 128,000hp, max. speed 30 knots
Dimensions	Length: 780ft 3in Beam 107ft 5in

Zara Class Cruisers	
Displacement	14,000 tons
Crew	841
Armament	8 x 8in & 16 x 4.1in guns
Armour	Max: 150mm
Engine	Two turbines, 95,000hp, max. speed 32 knots
Dimensions	Length: 557ft 2in Beam 62ft 10in

Vittorio Veneto *Class
battleship* Littorio

4 Italian Aircraft

When entering the war, the Regia Aeronautica thought that there was still a place for highly manoeuvrable biplane fighters, and the Fiat CR.42 Falco was the world's last and possibly the best, but it was soon outclassed by modern monoplane designs.

Italian wartime aircraft were generally no more than mediocre and always deficient in gun armament and bomb load. Some types could only be described, operationally speaking, as complete failures.

However the Macchi MC.200 was an admirable fighter with great agility and superb handling qualities, comparable with the British Hurricane. The graceful MC.202 Folgore was also a good fighter, but the armament proved insufficient when compared to its combat foes. The best Italian fighter of the war was the MC.205 Veltro, which could meet the North American P-51D Mustang on equal terms.

Italian bombers were generally poor and outdated; Italy's best and most important bomber of WW2 was the Savoia-Marchetti S.M.79 Sparviero. It was a rugged aircraft, and proved to be an outstanding torpedo-bomber, sinking numerous Allied warships and taking a heavy toll of merchant ships.

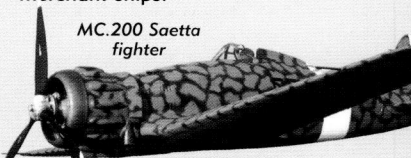

MC.200 Saetta fighter

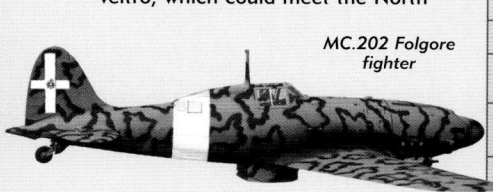

MC.202 Folgore fighter

Macchi MC.200 Saetta	
Weight	5,710lb
Crew	One
Armament	Two 12.7mm machine-guns
Range	540 miles
Engine	Fiat, 870hp, max. speed 312mph
Dimensions	Length: 26ft 10in. Wing span: 34ft 8in. Height: 11ft 6in
Production	1,153

Macchi MC.202 Folgore	
Weight	6,475lb
Crew	One
Armament	Two 12.7mm machine-guns and two 7.7mm machine-guns
Range	475 miles
Engine	Alfa Romeo, 1,175hp, max. speed 370mph
Dimensions	Length: 29ft 0in. Wing span: 34ft 9in. Height: 9ft 11in
Production	1,100

S.M.79 Sparviero	
Weight	23,100lb
Crew	Four to five
Armament	Two 12.7mm machine-guns and two 7.7mm machine-guns, bomb-load 2,750lb
Range	1,180 miles
Engine	Three Alfa Romeo, 780hp, max. speed 267mph
Dimensions	Length: 51ft 10in. Wing span: 69ft 7in. Height: 14ft 2in
Production	1,370

S.M.79 Sparviero bomber

The Japanese soldier could be fanatical in combat, being instilled with the samurai code of *Bushido* and absolute loyalty to the Japanese Emperor. Death before surrender was the accepted norm.

In 1941 the Japanese Army had 51 divisions and numbered 1,700,000 men. It was mostly stationed in China and Manchuria. The Japanese had occupied Manchuria in 1931 and then attacked China in 1937. In China they were engaged by both the Nationalist Chinese forces and the Communists. At the beginning of 1942 the various Japanese Armies began to go on the offensive in the Pacific, conquering Hong Kong, the Philippines, Thailand, Burma, the Dutch East Indies and Malaya. The Japanese Army performed superbly in the early stages of the Pacific conflict and had gained control over a huge geographical area that extended from the borders of India in the west to New Guinea in the south, all within six months.

The turning point in the Pacific War came in the summer of 1942 as the US went on the offensive. As the war progressed, the Japanese Army suffered heavily in losses of matériel, territory and men. But every piece of territory that they defended exacted a price paid on both sides, and it was always high in terms of the lives of

Japanese troops celebrating a victory

the soldiers fighting. Notable among the battles were those for Iwo Jima and Okinawa.

By 1945 there were 5.5 million men in the Japanese Army. If the two atomic bombs had not been dropped and if the Japanese government had not surrendered, the Allies would have had to invade the Japanese home islands, possibly in November 1945. The dedication shown by the Japanese soldier in defence of lands other than his own would have been as nothing compared to the ferocity he would have undoubtedly have shown in the defence of his homeland.

Japanese troops

When Japan attacked Pearl Harbor she had ten battleships, ten aircraft carriers, 38 cruisers, 112 destroyers and 65 submarines – a very well trained and formidable Navy. Of the 451 warships Japan eventually commissioned during the war, 332 were sunk. Japan always lagged behind the Allies with regard to vital technological advances such as radar and ASDIC but made up for this with superior combat skills, such as night gunnery and the use of very long-range torpedoes. For the first six months of the fighting the Japanese Navy swept all before it until the defeat at the Battle of Midway.

The mighty *Yamato* and *Musashi* were the largest battleships ever built, but they eventually fell foul of US Navy warplanes and were sunk by them. Three other battleships were sunk in the same way, another three by US warships, another by a combination of aircraft and warships and one by submarine.

Japan's powerful cruisers had some striking successes during the early part of the conflict, the heavy cruisers being particularly formidable, but by the

Takao Class Cruisers	
Displacement	15,000 tons
Crew	773
Armament	10 x 8in, 4 x 4.7in guns
Armour	Max: 127mm. Min: 13mm
Engine	Four turbines, 130,000hp, max. speed 27 knots
Dimensions	Length: 668ft 6in Beam 59ft 2in

Cruiser Takao

Kagero Class Destroyers	
Displacement	2,500 tons
Crew	240
Armament	6 x 5in guns & 8 x 24in torpedo tubes
Engine	Two turbines, 52,000hp, max. speed 35 knots
Dimensions	Length: 388ft 9in Beam 35ft 5in

Kagero *Class Destroyer*

Yamato Class Battleships	
Displacement	70,000 tons
Crew	2,500
Armament	9 x 18.1in, 12 x 6.1in guns
Armour	Max: 545mm. Min: 200mm
Engine	Four turbines, 150,000hp, max. speed 27 knots
Dimensions	Length: 862ft 11in Beam 121ft 1in

war's end 41 of their number had been sunk and only two remained afloat.

The same can be said for the destroyer force which was equipped with some very potent ships. It was in the thick of the fighting, but eventually it succumbed to the US Navy, losing 106 of the 126 that eventually entered service.

Battleship Yamato

The Japanese aircraft carrier force conducted the spectacularly successful raid on Pearl Harbor on December 7, 1941. All eight battleships of the US Pacific Fleet were either sunk or badly damaged, plus two cruisers and two destroyers. The raid was inspired by the British Fleet Air Arm's attack on the Italian fleet at Taranto on November 11, 1940.

The Imperial Japanese Navy carriers were the spearhead of a dramatic series of naval victories during the first six months of the Pacific war, but at the Battle of the Coral Sea they lost their first carrier. Then,

Kaga	
Displacement	30,000 tons
Crew	1,340
Armament	60 aircraft
Engine	Four turbines, 91,000hp, max. speed 27.5 knots
Dimensions	Length: 782ft 6in Beam: 100ft 0in

Carrier Kaga

three carriers. Japanese carrier-borne air power was now practically non-existent. The final humiliation came at the Battle of Cape Engano, on October 25, 1944, where the remaining carriers were used only as decoys because of their lack of trained aircrew; four more carriers were lost. Japan completed 22 aircraft carriers during the war, losing 19. One of the main Japanese failings was that they did not have an aircrew training system capable of keeping up with losses. The US Navy did, and provided for expansion.

Ryujo	
Displacement	8,000 tons
Crew	600
Armament	48 aircraft
Engine	Two turbines, 65,000hp, max. speed 29 knots
Dimensions	Length: 590ft 3in Beam: 75ft 6in

Carrier Ryujo

one month later, the loss of four carriers at the Battle of Midway on June 4, 1942, was a real disaster, compounded by the loss of so many irreplaceable Japanese aircrew. There then followed a series of defeats and losses. Then, at the Battle of the Philippine Sea on June 19–20, 1944, Japan received another body blow, the loss of another

Shokaku Class	
Displacement	32,000 tons
Crew	1,660
Armament	84 aircraft
Engine	Four turbines, 160,000hp, max. speed 34 knots
Dimensions	Length: 844ft 10in Beam: 95ft 1in

Shokaku *Class carrier*

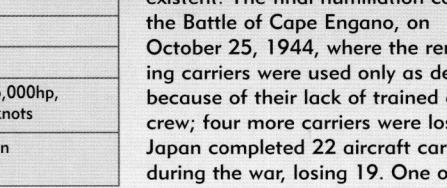

4 Japanese Aircraft

Japanese Navy aircraft bore the brunt of the air fighting of the Pacific Campaign and among them were some excellent designs. In particular, the 'Zero' fighter outclassed all the Allied fighters facing it in terms of range, agility and speed during 1941/42. Dive- and torpedo-bombers were similarly well advanced at that stage of the war. These aircraft were blessed with a particularly long range, as was necessary when flying over the Pacific Ocean, but at the expense of protection for fuel tanks and sufficient armour, in order to save weight.

The Imperial Japanese Army Air Force was also equipped with some good aircraft. Notable fighters were the Kawasaki Hien 'Tony' and the Nakajima Hayate 'Frank'. The latter was the JAAF's finest fighter of the Pacific War. Entering service in August 1944, and though fighting against overwhelming odds, it acquitted itself very well.

Japanese bombers were all good, long-range aircraft but had limited bomb-carrying capacity and because they lacked protection were vulnerable to the Allied fighters' fire power. Japan even had its own rocket powered fighter based on the German Me 163, but it never enter into service before the war ended.

Mitsubishi A6M 'Zero'	
Weight	6,000lb
Crew	One
Armament	Two 20mm cannon and two 7.7mm machine-guns
Range	1,200 miles
Engine	Nakajima, 1,130hp, max. speed 350mph
Dimensions	Length: 29ft 11in. Wing span: 39ft 4in Height: 11ft 6in
Production	11,283 (all marks)

'Zero' fighter

'Kate' level/torpedo bomber

Nakajima B5N 'Kate'	
Weight	9,000lb
Crew	Three
Armament	One 7.7mm machine-gun and 1,764lb bomb-load/torpedo
Range	1,200 miles
Engine	Nakajima, 1,000hp, max. speed 235mph
Dimensions	Length: 33ft 9in. Wing span: 50ft 11in Height: 12ft 1in
Production	1,149

Mitsubishi G4M 'Betty'	
Weight	27,500lb
Crew	Seven
Armament	One 20mm cannon and four 7.7mm machine-guns, 2,200lb bomb-load
Range	3,700 miles (max.)
Engine	2 Mitsubishi, 1,800hp, max. speed 272mph
Dimensions	Length: 65ft 7in. Wing span: 82ft 0in Height: 19ft 8in
Production	2,446 (all marks)

'Betty' bomber

Kamikaze

In 1281 Japan was threatened with a Mongol invasion. When it seemed that the invading Mongol fleet was about to overwhelm the Japanese, a huge typhoon arose, destroying the Mongols. This typhoon that saved Japan became known as the *Kamikaze* or 'Divine Wind'. Late in World War II it was apparent that Japan was losing the war. With a last-ditch effort to turn the tide on their flagging fortunes, the Japanese resorted to suicide tactics and titled these *Kamikaze*.

Kamikaze pilots

Organised into 'Special Attack' groups, *Kamikaze* pilots used their aircraft, mostly fighters loaded with bombs, to crash into enemy ships, killing themselves and hopefully sinking the ship. Bushido enabled these pilots to come to terms with this form of attack and embrace their death.

Japan also developed a number of specialised suicide weapons such as the *Baka*. This rocket-powered, piloted missile was carried to within 50 miles of the target by a medium bomber. After being dropped it would glide towards the target, then, activating its rockets' engines, increase its speed and dive into the target, exploding its one-ton warhead. The *Baka*, once in flight, was difficult to stop, but its mother plane was extremely vulnerable to marauding US fighters and many were caught before they reached their targets.

There were also explosive motor torpedo boats, human torpedoes and midget submarines but these never proved as successful as aircraft in attacking ships. *Kamikaze* tactics were also employed against US B-29 bombers.

The first *Kamikaze* attacks occurred in June 1944, and they reached their zenith in April 1945 during the Allies' invasion of Okinawa, sinking 36 ships and landing vessels and damaging 368.

These tactics would have been very much part of the Japanese defence of their home islands in the event of an invasion.

The carrier USS Bunker Hill after being hit by a Kamikaze

Finnish Forces

The Soviet Union crossed the border with democratic Finland on November 30, 1939. The inadequately equipped Finnish Army consisted of ten divisions with fewer than 200,000 soldiers, but it was prepared for the Soviet invasion, utilising the sub-zero temperatures, the deep snow and the densely wooded terrain which greatly favoured defence. The Finns lacked modern communications equipment, anti-tank guns, anti-aircraft guns and motor transport. The well-trained and aggressive Finnish ski-troops could move freely through the snow-bound wilderness, and, even though greatly outnumbered, they fought particularly well. The Soviets would use 26 divisions consisting of 1,200,000 troops supported by 1,500 tanks and 3,000 aircraft.

The Finns' main defence was the Mannerheim Line, which managed to hold out until February 12, 1940. When it was finally breached the Finns had no alternative but to sue for peace, and they lost about 10% of their territory. The Finns had inflicted huge numbers of casualties on the Red Army, estimated at about

Britain supplied 30 Gloster Gladiator fighters to Finland

200,000. Finnish losses were about 25,000 killed and 45,000 wounded.

The Finnish Air Force had 200 aircraft, of which only about half were operational. Despite its weakness, it fought very well and inflicted heavy losses on the Soviet Air Force, estimated at over 200 aircraft.

Sweden aided her neighbour by contributing a squadron of aircraft and two battalions of infantry.

The Finns regained the lost territory when they joined with the Germans in the attack on the USSR in 1941. In an armistice concluded in September 1944 the Soviets demanded heavy reparations from Finland but the Finns did manage to save themselves from Soviet occupation and their democracy remained intact.

Finnish ski troop

The British Army had a strength of less than 900,000 Regular and Territorial soldiers when war was declared in September 1939.

The British Expeditionary Force (BEF) began to cross to France that same month. It was initially composed of four infantry divisions with 50 light tanks, but by May 1940 six more divisions had arrived and it now totalled over 390,000 men. Tank strength had grown to 300. On May 14, 1940 the Germans attacked and the BEF quickly became almost surrounded. It withdrew to Dunkirk and was evacuated across the Channel, back to Britain, with over 338,000 men,

Eighth Army anti-tank gunners

including 53,000 French. Another 136,000 were evacuated from other ports. They left 64,000 vital military vehicles and nearly 2,500 artillery pieces behind in France.

The Eighth Army was formed in September 1941, from the Western Desert Force that had defeated the Italians in North Africa. It included

British troops about to fire a mortar

many units from the Empire. After losing ground against the Afrika Korps it won the Second Battle of El Alamein in November 1942 and eventually participated in the ejection of the Axis forces from North Africa. It then participated in the Italian campaign, fighting its way eventually into Austria. It had distinguished itself fighting in the difficult conditions of North Africa and Italy.

Churchill tank

The Second Army was formed in 1943 and after the landings in Normandy in 1944 it fought through France, Belgium, the Netherlands and into Germany.

The worst defeat suffered by the British during the war was at Singapore where 130,000 British and colonial troops surrendered to the Japanese in February 1942.

The Fourteenth and then the Twelfth Armies fought during the long campaign and reconquest of Burma.

In terms of its military structure, each British army was divided into corps, a unit of approximately 30,000 troops and composed of two or more divisions. The division consisted of 10,000–15,000 soldiers of several different brigades, each with a strength ranging between 1,500 and 3,500. The brigade consisted of three or more battalion-size units.

The first half of the war taught the British Army some very harsh lessons in modern warfare and a series of sobering defeats were suffered, but after the victory in North Africa the majority of British battles led to victory.

Shortfalls in British equipment were made up with the huge quantities of American equipment that became available. British innovations, however, included the Sten submachine-gun, which was particularly cheap and simple to manufacture and was produced in large numbers.

At its peak the British Army had 11 armoured divisions, 34 infantry divisions and two airborne divisions. Over 3½ million men and women had enlisted, of whom 144,000 were killed, 240,000 were wounded and 152,000 made prisoners of war. A great many colonial troops fought within the British Army's structure.

Sten gun

British Tanks

4

British tank design at the early stages of World War II generally equalled that of Germany. However, as the war progressed, British tanks proved to be too lightly armed when compared with their German counterparts.

The Matilda Infantry Tank of the early war period was slow and poorly armed but heavily armoured, and proved to be difficult to knock out. The cruiser tanks were much faster but too lightly armoured and often mechanically unreliable. Later British tanks (e.g. the Cromwell) were much more reliable, but still too lightly armed and armoured. By 1941 the British began to supplement their tank stocks with American models.

During the war years Britain produced a total of over 25,000 tanks compared to Germany's 23,500.

Valentine Infantry Tank

Weight	18 tons
Crew	Three/four
Armament	2pdr or 6pdr gun (later a 75mm gun) and one 7.92mm BESA machine-gun
Armour	Max: 65mm. Min: 8mm
Engine	AEC, 135hp, speed 15mph
Dimensions	Length: 17ft 9in. Width: 8ft 7in. Height: 7ft 5in
Production	8,275

Valentine Tank

Crusader Tank

Crusader Cruiser Tank

Weight	20 tons
Crew	Three, four or five (dependent on mark)
Armament	2pdr or 6pdr gun and two 7.92 mm BESA MGs
Armour	Max: 51mm. Min: 7mm
Engine	Nuffield Liberty, 340hp, speed 27mph
Dimensions	Length: 19ft 8in. Width: 8ft 8in. Height: 7ft 4in
Production	5,300

Comet Cruiser Tank

Weight	35.5 tons
Crew	Five
Armament	One 77mm gun and two 7.92mm BESA machine-guns
Armour	Max: 102mm. Min: 14mm
Engine	Rolls-Royce, 600hp, speed 32mph
Dimensions	Length: 25ft 1in. Width: 10ft 0in. Height: 9ft 9in
Production	1,200

Comet Tank

Churchill tank in the Western Desert

ARMED FORCES **Great Britain**

British Capital Ships

On September 3, 1939, and the outbreak of war, the Royal Navy was the largest navy in the world. It had in commission fifteen battleships and battlecruisers, with another five battleships being built. It had seven aircraft carriers, with another four having been laid down at the builders' yards. Within weeks the carrier *Courageous* was sunk by a U-boat. The battleship *Royal Oak* was sunk by another U-boat less than a month later.

A total of five battleships were sunk out of the 20 that saw service. The most heartfelt loss was that of HMS *Hood*, the pride of the fleet, which blew up as a result of gunfire from the German battleship

Illustrious Class Carrier

Displacement	28,000 tons
Crew	1,200
Armament	36 aircraft
Engine	Three turbines, 111,000hp, max. speed 30 knots
Dimensions	Length: 743ft 3in Beam: 95ft 9in

Illustrious *Class carrier*
HMS Indomitable

King George V Class Battleship

Displacement	42,000 tons
Crew	1,422
Armament	10 x 14in, 16 x 5.25in guns
Armour	Max: 380mm. Min: 38mm
Engine/motor	Four turbines, 110,000hp, max. speed 28 knots
Dimensions	Length: 745ft 0in Beam: 103ft 0in

Battleship HMS
Duke of York

Bismarck. Two were sunk by U-boats and two by aircraft. 52 aircraft carriers saw service, this figure including 36 small escort types. Eight carriers were lost, five to U-boats, one to enemy surface ships, one to aircraft

Battlecruiser
HMS Hood

and one to an accidental fire on board.

British carriers and battleships played a crucial part in the war. Some notable successes were the aircraft carrier HMS *Illustrious*'s attack on the Italian fleet at Taranto and the crippling of three battleships. A vital part was played by HMS *Formidable* at the Battle of Matapan, where her aircraft slowed the Italian warships and led to their sinking by three British battleships. *Ark Royal* crippled the *Bismarck*, leading to her eventual destruction by British battleships. HMS *Duke of York*'s use of her big guns brought about the destruction of the German battleship *Scharnhorst*. Battleships and escort carriers also had a vital role in escorting convoys. The escort carriers, in particular, played a very important part in the final defeat of the U-boats.

British battleships' big guns were also used to telling effect in shore bombardment, particularly on D-Day and the battle for Normandy.

A total of 86 cruisers saw service with the Royal Navy during the course of hostilities, and during the six years 27 were lost and 29 new ships completed. They were heavily engaged in all the major fleet actions involving the RN, and also hunted down commerce raiders and undertook convoy escort and protection. Typical were the Town Class. They were well balanced, well armed and good fighting ships.

Nearly 380 destroyers saw British service, including the 50 old US destroyers handed over to the British as part of 'Lend Lease'. Over 100 ships were lost. The destroyers were the RN's workhorses, accounting for scores of U-boats and enemy aircraft as well as some major enemy warships. They were ships called upon for escorting and fighting through even the smallest and hard-pressed of convoys, as well as escorting the most prestigious capital ships.

But the RN's unsung heroes of the war were the slow sloops, frigates and corvettes, which numbered well over a thousand. They performed the gruelling and tedious duty of ocean as well as coastal convoy escort and often more efficiently than the more glamourous destroyer.

Tribal Class Destroyers	
Displacement	2,000 tons
Crew	190
Armament	8 x 4.7in guns, 4 x 21in torpedo tubes
Engine	Two turbines, 44,000hp, max. speed 36 knots
Dimensions	Length: 377ft 6in Beam 36ft 6in

Tribal Class destroyer HMS Maori

Flower Class corvette

Town Class Cruisers	
Displacement	11,000tons
Crew	850
Armament	12 x 6in, 8 x 4in guns
Armour	Max: 114mm. Min: 25mm
Engine	Four turbines 75,000hp max. speed 32 knots
Dimensions	Length: 591ft 6in Beam 61ft 8in

Town Class cruiser HMS Gloucester

Flower Class Corvettes	
Displacement	925 tons
Crew	85
Armament	1 x 4in & 1 x 2pdr AA guns plus depth charges
Engine	Four cylinder 2,750hp engine, max. speed 16 knots
Dimensions	Length: 190ft 0in Beam 33ft 0in

RAF Aircraft

RAF Fighter Command started the war with two very good fighters, the Hurricane and the Spitfire. The Spitfire was progressively updated and improved and went through a total of 24 marks. At first the RAF bomber force was equipped with a diverse collection of bombers. Apart from the Wellington, these aircraft – Battle, Blenheim, Whitley and Hampden – were a disappointment, and all were only light or medium bombers.

As the war progressed capable new fighters joined the fray, such as the Hawker Typhoon, the Tempest and the Allies' first jet, the Gloster Meteor. When the big four-engined bombers started to join Bomber Command, firstly the Stirling then the Lancaster and Halifax, the RAF had the ability to bring about the devastation of Germany's cities and her industry.

The de Havilland Mosquito became the world's first truly multi-role warplane. Largely built of wood, this aircraft could operate as a high-speed bomber, fighter and night fighter reconnaissance type.

Supermarine Spitfire

Supermarine Spitfire Mk IX

Weight	9,500lb (fully loaded)
Crew	One
Armament	Two 20mm cannon and four .303in machine-guns
Range	980 miles
Engine	Rolls-Royce Merlin, 1,565hp, max speed 408mph
Dimensions	Length: 31ft 0in. Wing Span: 36ft 10in. Height: 12ft 7in
Production	20,351 (all marks)

Hawker Hurricane

Avro Lancaster

Weight	65,000lb (fully loaded)
Crew	Seven
Armament	Eight .303in machine-guns, bomb-load 18,000lb
Range	2,500 miles
Engine	4 Rolls-Royce Merlins, 1,640hp, max speed 245mph
Dimensions	Length: 69ft 6in. Wing span: 102ft 0in. Height: 21ft 0in
Production	7,378 (all marks)

Hawker Hurricane Mk I

Weight	6,218lb (fully loaded)
Crew	One
Armament	Eight .303in machine-guns
Range	525 miles
Engine	Rolls-Royce Merlin, 1,030hp, max speed 308mph
Dimensions	Length: 31ft 4in Wing Span: 40ft 0in Height: 13ft 4in
Production	14,232 (all marks)

Avro Lancaster

The Home Guard

In Britain the Local Defence Volunteers (LDV) were raised on May 14, 1940 and within 24 hours 250,000 men had volunteered. 'Dad's Army', as it was affectionately called, allowed men too old, exempt or unsuitable for general military duty to 'do their bit' for King and country.

At first equipment was very scarce, weapons improvised and organisation haphazard. The Home Guard, as it was now renamed, had received large quantities of weapons from the USA by July 1940 just as the justifiable fears of invasion were at their most intense. They performed the useful, if somewhat humble tasks, of guarding factories, the coastline and of establishing roadblocks. Some even experienced the excitement of rounding up Luftwaffe crews whose aircraft had been shot down. This allowed the Regular Army, after Dunkirk, to reform and concentrate on re-equipping and training.

Uniforms and equipment started to filter through, and by the summer of 1943 the Home Guard was a well-equipped force with a strength of 1¾ million and an average age of under

Home Guardsmen about to communicate by carrier pigeon

30. Many manned anti-aircraft batteries, thereby playing an active combat role. The Home Guard was useful training for boys aged 17 and 18 before their call-up and joining the regular armed forces.

When the Home Guard stood down in December 1944 many members were disappointed that it had to finish as it had become a way of life for many as well as a form of hobby.

LDV at rifle practice

Dominion Forces

The countries of the British Empire covered one quarter of the world's land surface. From the Caribbean, African, Indian, and all the other colonies, troops and personnel played a crucial role in supporting the Allied cause in World War II.

Over one million Canadians enlisted in the armed forces. Of these, 42,000 were killed and over 54,000 were wounded. As well as sending troops to the UK, the Canadians sent them to assist in the defence of Hong Kong. In August of 1942, at the tragic débâcle at Dieppe, over half of the 5,000 Canadians involved were lost. Large numbers were present in Sicily, Italy and the invasion of Europe, where the Canadian 1st Army fought through to the enemy's surrender in Germany. Many Canadian airmen served with the RAF making their greatest contribution in Bomber Command. The Royal Canadian Navy made a huge contribution to winning the Battle of the Atlantic, as well as serving on many of the other naval fronts.

During the war nearly one million Australians enlisted in the armed

forces. Nearly 27,000 died and 24,000 were wounded. The Army fought particularly well in the North African, Balkan and Syrian campaigns and against the Japanese in Malaya, New Guinea and Borneo. The Royal Australian Navy made a considerable contribution to the sea battles in the Mediterranean and in the South Pacific campaigns. Australian airmen served in the RAF as well as the RAAF, seeing action in Europe, the Middle East, Malaya and the South Pacific.

As a ratio of her population, New Zealand suffered the greatest numbers killed among all the member countries of the Empire – over 11,500 out of a population of less than 1¾ million, along with nearly 16,000 wounded. The New Zealanders fought in much the same campaigns as their fellow ANZACs, the Australians.

At the start of the war the Indian Army comprised 350,000 professional volunteers but by the end of the conflict this had risen to 2½ million – the largest volunteer army in history. It

Australian troops about to embark for Egypt

The New Zealand cruiser Achilles *was one of the warships that fought at the Battle of the River Plate*

suffered 24,000 killed and 64,000 wounded. Indian troops fought in North Africa, East Africa, Italy, Syria, Iraq, Malaya and Hong Kong, and of particular note was their victory in Burma against the Japanese.

South Africa raised nearly 335,000 volunteers, losing nearly 9,000 dead and over 8,000 wounded. The South Africans fought against the Axis in the North and East African campaigns, as well as in Italy. Many South African airmen fought with the RAF and SAAF squadrons, fighting in Madagascar and the Central Mediterranean, and for a while they made up almost one third of the strike power of the Western Desert Air Force.

Indian troops in training

US Army

The US Army in September 1939 had a strength of 190,000. By the end of the war it had a strength in excess of 6,000,000 – a relatively small army when compared with size of the population and with that of other nations.

Eleven different field armies were deployed during the course of the war. The First, Third, Seventh, Ninth and Fifteenth Armies fought in North-West Europe, the Fifth in Italy and the Sixth, Eighth and Tenth Armies in the Pacific. The Second and Fourth Armies were stationed in the USA on training and administrative duties. Each Army consisted of two or more corps, of which 26 were formed in total. They each usually consisted of three divisions, plus ancillary units.

The basic fighting formation was the division, and during the course of the war 90 divisions were deployed, 68 in Europe and 22 in the Pacific. The

majority were infantry divisions. Each division had approximately 14,500 men of three regiments of three battalions,

Four-wheel-drive Willys Jeep, of which over 650,000 were built

plus supporting arms. Sixteen of these were armoured divisions and these had an established strength of 263 tanks, but three – the 1st, 2nd and 3rd Armored Divisions – had 390 tanks. The armoured divisions were all deployed to Europe. There they suffered badly due to the superiority of

An M3 half-track and an M4 Sherman tank

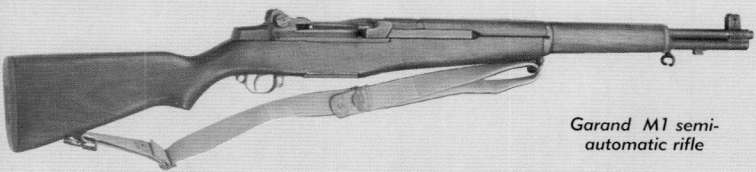

A 'Deuce and a Half' 2½ ton truck, of which over 750,000 were built

German tanks and anti-tank weaponry they were fighting against, but eventually they won through. The main US tank, the Sherman, was reliable, but it was too lightly armed and armoured.

Tanks were important during mobile offensive warfare but, as General Patton said, it was the US artillery that gave the infantry and tanks the necessary edge over their enemy.

Five airborne divisions were raised, the 13th, 11th, 17th, 82nd and 101st. These élite units had fewer troops – less than 13,000 or, in the case of the 11th, only 8,500.

Generally the GI was the best-equipped soldier of the war. American technological innovation and manufacturing techniques not only supplied him with good equipment, but also a vast range and large quantities of it. Such items as the M1 Garand semi-automatic rifle, the GMC 2½-ton truck and the ubiquitous Willys Jeep were war winners.

During the early part of the fighting the inexperienced US Army had some hard lessons to learn, being opposed by the battle-hardened Japanese and Germans. The early loss of the Philippines and the mauling the GIs received at the battle for the Kasserine Pass in Tunisia in 1942 not only caused the loss of men and *matériel* but generated a loss of confidence. But the lessons were gradually learnt and the war was won.

The US Army fought in 34 specific campaigns, suffering over 820,000 casualties, including nearly 183,000 killed.

Garand M1 semi-automatic rifle

US Tanks

The US seriously neglected tank development between the two world wars, but with the outbreak of conflict in Europe in 1939 there was an expansion of tank production which eventually became phenomenal: between July 1940 and the war's end production totalled over 88,000.

The bulk of the USA's production was taken up by the M4 Sherman, which served with all the main Allied forces, including the Soviets.

US tanks proved to be not only very reliable but (especially in the case of the Sherman) also adaptable, and could be upgraded in a desperate attempt to match the ever more powerful tanks of the German Army. However, the sheer quantity of US tanks proved to be the war winner.

M3 Lee/ Grant

M3 'Lee/Grant' Medium Tank

Weight	27 tons
Crew	Six
Armament	75mm gun, one 37mm gun and 3 or 4 .30in Browning machine-guns
Armour	Max: 50mm. Min: 13mm
Engine	Wright Continental, 340hp, speed 32mph
Dimensions	Length: 18ft 6in. Width: 8ft 11in. Height: 10ft 4in
Production	4,924

M4 Sherman

M4 Sherman Medium Tank

Weight	30 tons
Crew	Five
Armament	75mm gun, one .50in and three .30in Browning machine-guns
Armour	Max: 51mm. Min: 19mm
Engine	Wright Continental, 400hp, speed 25mph
Dimensions	Length: 19ft 2in. Width: 8ft 9in. Height: 9ft 0in
Production	50,000

M26 Persh

M26 Pershing Heavy Tank

Weight	41 tons
Crew	Five
Armament	One 90mm gun, one .50in and two .30in Browning machine-guns
Armour	Max: 102mm. Min: 7mm
Engine	Ford V-8, 500hp, max. speed 20mph
Dimensions	Length: 28ft 10in. Width: 11ft 6in. Height: 9ft 1in
Production	2,428

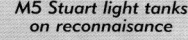

M5 Stuart light tanks on reconnaisance

The strength of the Marine Corps at the time of the Japanese attack on Pearl Harbor was 65,000, but by the end of the war it had risen to 450,000, incorporating six combat divisions. The Corps suffered over 90,000 casualties, of which 20,000 were killed.

The US Marines are a separate service within the US Navy, being the latter's land combat troops as well as having an autonomous amphibious operations role. It also had its own aviation with 10 squadrons at the start of the war and 132 squadrons at the end, flying bombing, fighter and tactical air support missions. The top-scoring USMC fighter ace was Gregory 'Pappy' Boyington, with 24 kills to his credit.

The *esprit de corps* of the US Marines is legendary. One of the USA's toughest military services, they were in continuous combat in the Pacific from the battle for Wake Island in December 1941 to Okinawa in June 1945. The Marines experienced some of the most gruelling battles of the entire conflict.

The Marine Corps began its development of modern amphibious warfare techniques working closely with the Navy. With the increasing experience of the amphibious assaults in the Pacific, the Marines became ever more proficient and the developing tactics were given ample chance to prove themselves during the assaults on Guadalcanal, Bougainville, Tarawa, Roi-Namur, Eniwetok, New Britain,

US Marines raise the Stars and Stripes on Mount Suribachi

Tinian, Guam, Peleliu, Iwo Jima and Okinawa.

The Iwo Jima battle cost the Marines about 20,000 casualties, the highest number suffered by the Corps in a single engagement. It epitomised the fighting spirit of the Corps. A very small Pacific island 650 miles south of Japan, it had strategic significance due to its proximity to the Japanese homeland. The Japanese turned the entire volcanic island into a labyrinth of large tunnels and fortifications. The battle was hard and the determination of the Japanese defenders implacable, only a handful of whom survived. When the Marines reached the summit of Mount Suribachi on February 23 the American flag was raised.

US Marines fighting at Bougainville

US Warships

When the the US was attacked at Pearl Harbor by the Japanese, the eight battleships of the Pacific Fleet were either sunk or badly damaged, but, apart from two, they were eventually repaired and returned to service. America had a total of 17 battleships when she started the war and 25 at the finish.

The most potent of the US Navy's battleships were the four ships of the *Iowa* Class. They remained in service until the mid-1990s, two firing their guns in anger for the last time during the 1991 Gulf War.

Iowa Class Battleships

Displacement	58,000 tons
Crew	1,921
Armament	9 x 16in, 20 x 5in guns
Armour	Max: 440mm. Min: 152mm
Engine	Four turbines, 212,000hp, max. speed 32 knots
Dimensions	Length: 887ft 3in Beam 108ft 2in

One hundred cruisers saw service with the USN during the war years, of which ten were sunk. The most numerous, and also the most typical, were the 38 ships of the *Cleveland*

Cleveland Class Cruisers

Displacement	14,000 tons
Crew	1,285
Armament	12 x 6in & 12 x 5in guns
Armour	Max: 165mm
Engine	Four turbines, 100,000hp, max. speed 32 knots
Dimensions	Length: 610ft 1in Beam 66ft 4in

Iowa Class battleship

Fletcher Class Destroyers

Displacement	2,900 tons
Crew	273
Armament	5 x 5in guns & 10 x 21in torpedo tubes
Engine/motor	Two turbines, 60,000hp, max. speed 38 knots
Dimensions	Length: 376ft 5in Beam 39ft 7in

Fletcher *Class destroyer*

Class. They were good all-round fighting ships, seeing much action from the Mediterranean and across the Pacific fighting to the final surrender of Japan, without the loss of a single ship of the class.

Of the 441 destroyers of the US Navy's fleet, 59 were lost. The most famous were the *Fletcher* Class which made up 176 of the total number of destroyers built; 19 were lost, predominantly to *Kamikaze* attack. Good all-round combat ships, they bore the brunt of much of the sea fighting against the Japanese, accounting directly for the sinking of ten Japanese destroyers and 21 submarines and assisting in the destruction of numerous other ships.

Cleveland *Class cruiser*

US Carrier Forces

The US used a total of 105 carriers, of which 72 were the small and slow escort carriers. Ten carriers of all types were lost. It was the fleet-type carriers that formed the striking force of the Navy and 17 of these were the excellent *Essex* Class. There were also nine light fleet carriers of the *Independence* Class. No *Essex* Class carriers were lost but several were badly damaged, typically by *Kamikazes*.

The Carrier Task Forces of the US Navy's Pacific Fleet were crucial to winning the war against Japan. Early examples were Task Forces 16 and 17, operating with just three fleet aircraft carriers during the Battle of Midway in June 1942.

Admiral Halsey's Third Fleet and Admiral Spruance's Fifth Fleet were merged in 1944, Spruance and Halsey taking it in turns to command. When Spruance was in command it was called the Fifth Fleet, with Halsey the Third Fleet. This was at the time the most powerful fleet in the world, the backbone being the fast carrier groups.

The doctrine of mass air strikes had evolved, employing hundreds of aircraft at the same time rather than dozens. At the US victory at the Battle of the Philippine Sea, in June 1944, Task Force 58 (the Fast Carrier Task Force) swept all before it. It consisted of five Task Groups. At the front was the Battle Line, Task Group 58.7, consisting of a large circle of seven battleships with associated cruisers and destroyers on picket duty. Slightly north of them was Task Group 58.4, with three carriers plus cruisers and destroyers. To the east were the three major carrier groups Task Groups 58.1, 58.2, 58.3, all with two fleet carriers and two light fleet carriers, plus attendant cruisers and destroyers. The carriers in each Task Group cruised in a diamond formation, surrounded by five cruisers and then by 12–15 destroyers in a four-mile circle around them, providing anti-submarine and anti-aircraft defence.

Independence *Class light fleet carrier*

Essex Class Carrier	
Displacement	30,000 tons
Crew	2,682
Armament	90 aircraft
Engine/motor	Four turbines, 150,000hp, max. speed 32 knots
Dimensions	Length: 872ft 0in Beam 96ft 0in

Independence Class Carrier	
Displacement	14,500 tons
Crew	1,569
Armament	30 aircraft
Engine/motor	Four turbines, 100,000hp, max. speed 31 knots
Dimensions	Length: 600ft 0in Beam 73ft 0in

Essex *Class fleet carriers, December 1944*

US Submarines

US Navy submarines played a decisive role in driving Japanese warships and merchant vessels from the Pacific Ocean. The US Navy conducted the most successful campaign of unrestricted submarine warfare against Japan, much superior to that which the Germans fought in the Atlantic against the Allies. During the fighting the Japanese merchant marine lost over 2,300 vessels, eight and a half million tons of shipping, US submarines accounting for five million tons of this – 1,300 ships. US submarines also sank over 600,000 tons of warships, nearly 30% of the total, including eight aircraft carriers, one battleship and eleven cruisers.

Of the total of 288 US submarines deployed throughout the war, 52 were lost, 48 of them in the Pacific. American submariners comprised some 1.6% of Navy personnel but suffered the highest loss rate in all the US Armed Forces, with 22% killed.

There were several early submarine classes, of mixed quality, serving with the US Navy during the war. The oldest was the S Class, a World War I design. There were also large fleet types, culminating in the 228 boats of the *Gato*, *Balao* and *Tench* Classes, which were the classic boats of the US Navy's wartime mass-production programmes. These three classes were virtually identical, and were, arguably, the finest submarines of the war.

USS Hackleback

Gato/Balao/Tench **Classes**	
Displacement	2,400 tons
Crew	80/81
Armament	6 x 21in torpedo tubes forward, 4 aft. 1–2 x 4in/5in guns and various AA guns
Engine/motor	5,400hp surfaced, 2,740hp submerged, max. speed surfaced 20 knots, submerged 8.75 knots
Dimensions	Length: 311ft 9in Beam 27ft 3in

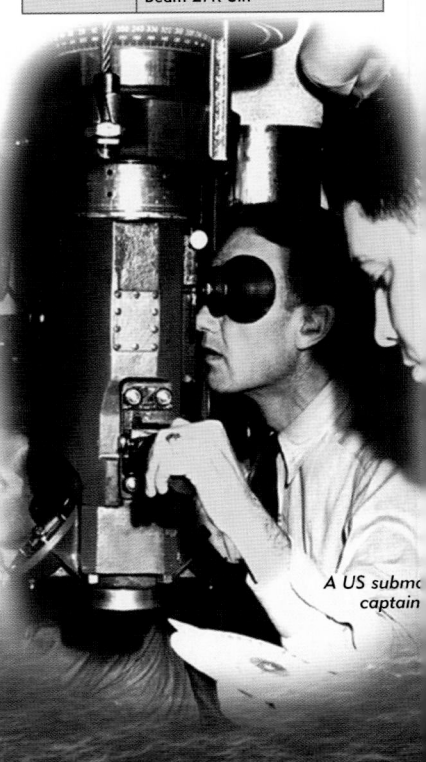

A US subma
captain

US Aircraft

4

ARMED FORCES USA

In late 1939 the USAAF had 2,500 aircraft of all types, many obsolescent. By mid-1944 it had nearly 80,000, of which most were the equal of, or better than, those of its opponents.

When the US entered the war it had few state-of-the-art fighters. Many were the tubby Brewster Buffalo or the disappointing Curtiss Hawk family of fighters. Better were the Wildcat and the twin-engined Lightning, which were able to hold their own against the enemy. It was with the arrival of fighters such as the P-47 Thunderbolt, the P-51 Mustang and the US Navy F6F Hellcat that the Allies would gain the air superiority needed to bring the Axis air-power to its knees. The combination of high speed, agility, long range and fire power made the Mustang arguably the best fighter of World War II. The Hellcat was credited with 6,000 enemy aircraft shot down, 75% of the total number of US Navy air-to-air victories.

In the medium bomber role, aircraft such as the ubiquitous B-25 Mitchell and the capable B-26 Marauder would effectively carry out tactical bombing. The heavy bombers, the B-17 Flying Fortress, B-24 Liberator and the B-29 Superfortress were for the longer-range strategic bombing attacks, playing their part in the devastation of German cities and industry and the razing to the ground of numerous Japanese cities.

North American P-51D Mustang

Weight	12,100lb (fully loaded)
Crew	One
Armament	Six 0.5in machine-guns
Range	1,650 miles
Engine	Packard Merlin, 1,400hp, max speed 437mph
Dimensions	Length: 32ft 3in Wing Span: 37ft 0in Height: 13ft 8in
Production	15,469 (all marks)

P-51D Mustang

Boeing B-17 Flying Fortress

Weight	55,000lb (fully loaded)
Crew	Ten
Armament	13 0.5in machine-guns, bomb-load 5,000lb
Range	3,400 miles
Engine	4 General Electric, 1,200hp max speed 300mph
Dimensions	Length: 74ft 9in Wing Span: 103ft 9in Height: 19ft 1in
Production	12,731 (all marks)

Grumman F6F Hellcat

Weight	15,400lb (fully loaded)
Crew	One
Armament	Six 0.5in machine-guns
Range	950 miles
Engine	Pratt and Whitney, 2,000hp, max speed 380mph
Dimensions	Length: 33ft 7in Wing Span: 42ft 10in Height: 13ft 1in
Production	12,275

Grumman F6F Hellcat

Boeing B-17G Flying Fortress

99

French Armed Forces

On September 3, 1939 France declared war on Germany and the French armed forces spent the next eight months, 'safe' behind the Maginot Line, in relative inactivity. The *Drôle de Guerre* (Phoney War) was suddenly broken on May 10, 1940 when the Germans invaded, and in less than six weeks France was conquered.

Numerically the French Army was superior to that of the Germans. Their tanks were good and they had more of them. The French High Command was, however, geared towards static warfare, the concept of defence and the Maginot Line. The Army was let down by tactics that were outdated and uninspired.

The French Air Force had inadequate equipment, and fewer than half of its 2,200 aircraft could be consid-

French artillery

Morane-Saulnier MS.406 fighter

ered modern. Consequently it was annihilated by the Luftwaffe.

The French Navy was highly respected in 1939–40. It was the fourth largest in the world and many of its ships were modern. Until the collapse it had operated with distinction, but the French warships at Mers-el-Kébir would not join with the British to continue the fight against the Germans so, reluctantly, the Royal Navy had to attack them in order to stop these powerful vessels from falling into German hands. As a consequence French ships were sunk and many French sailors lost their lives.

140,000 personnel of the Free French Forces, commanded by Charles de Gaulle, stood alongside the Allies. They continued the fight against the Germans and following D-Day and the victory in Normandy in 1944 they were the troops that liberated their capital, Paris, from the Nazi oppressors.

Heavy cruiser Algérie

When the Germans invaded the USSR (Operation 'Barbarossa') in June 1941, the Red Army on paper seemed impressive with nearly 5½ million troops plus another 5 million reservists. They possessed 20,000 tanks, of which 1,800 were the latest KV or T-34 types and superior to the best the German Army had. The invading army had just over 3½ million men and 3,600 tanks. The Red Army forces should have been sufficiently capable of repelling any aggressor.

The largest Soviet army formation was the front: this controlled between five to seven armies, which were each made up of several corps of between three to nine divisions. A division, depending on type, consisted of a brigade of four regiments each of three battalions, plus an anti-aircraft battalion.

The 61 Red Army tank divisions (10,500 troops) would each have 375 tanks, twice as many as the equivalent Panzer formation. A rifle (infantry) division had nearly three times as many machine-guns as a German infantry division. The Red Army raised 400 divisions during the war.

Serious shortcomings within the Soviet Army first became apparent during its invasion of Finland in November 1939. The purges and executions of the officer class by the paranoid Stalin during 1937–38 had rendered the Army poorly trained and inefficient with regard to leadership.

There seemed to be nothing the Soviet Army could do to halt the German *Blitzkrieg*. In the great encirclement battles of 1941, 26 Soviet armies were destroyed, the Germans taking over 2 million Soviet troops as prisoners of war and also capturing 7,500 tanks and 13,000 artillery pieces. The trend continued into 1942 with another 11 armies eliminated and 600,000 prisoners, 2,500 tanks and 4,500 guns taken. The number of Soviets killed and wounded was appaling as each Soviet counter-offensive achieved nothing and the German advance continued.

In the summer of 1942 the Soviets began to form complete Tank Armies, each comprising two tank corps plus all the ancillary units, aimed purely at massive offensive operations. These Soviet 'steamroller' tactics were not

Snow-camouflaged Soviet troops advancing

KV-1 tanks, paid for by donations from collective farmers, being presented to Soviet troops

the most subtle, as they had to be able to absorb huge numbers of casualties. This is what Stalin exploited. The Soviets had an abundance of men and factories, which were now turning out ever more tanks and guns with which to arm them.

The Red Army soldier's equipment was simple, cheap and usually reliable but crudely manufactured. If it was damaged or broke down one simply replaced it – one of the joys of mass production on a huge scale.

Despite the setbacks, the Soviet soldier continued to defend stubbornly and with growing skill and improved leadership during the winter of 1942/43 the tide was turned at Stalingrad. The Soviets succeeded in

surrounding and eliminating the 20 divisions of the German Sixth Army, consisting of nearly 250,000 men. They then defeated the big German summer offensive of 1943 at the great tank battle of Kursk.

The Soviet Army would not taste retreat again as the 'steamroller' began to push the enemy steadily back – all the way to the gates of Berlin by April 1945.

Throughout the war the Soviet Army's losses were extremely high: in the region of ten million servicemen were killed and 18 million wounded, and over five million were taken prisoner. Tank losses were enormous, with nearly 100,000 destroyed or captured.

The crudely produced but very effective PPSh 41 sub-machine gun. It could be fitted either with a 35-round box-magazine or a 71-round drum magazine

When they entered the war the Russians had the largest tank force in the world but, owing to military incompetence, they lost some 17,500 to the 2,500 Panzers of the German Army during the first months of the fighting.

The early T-26 and BT-7 series of tanks were of good design, as were most other Soviet tanks apart from the large multi-turreted T-35 and the giant KV-2.

Soviet tanks were crudely built compared with their German counterparts. Even so, the T-34 series of tanks can be considered as possibly

the best all-round tanks of the war, possessing good speed, reliability, protection and firepower and being simple to maintain.

The KV-1 took the Germans by surprise at the start of Operation 'Barbarossa'. It was virtually invulnerable to German anti-tank gun fire other than from the 88. Its successor, the IS-2 'Stalin', could even challenge the mighty Tiger tank on even terms.

T-34 Tank

Weight	28 tons (T-34/85 32 tons)
Crew	Four
Armament	76.2mm gun (later 85mm) and two 7.62mm MG
Armour	Max: 47mm. Min: 16mm
Engine	V-2 V-12, 500hp, speed 32mph
Dimensions	Length: 21ft 7in. Width: 9ft 10in. Height: 8ft 0in
Production	40,000

T-34/85 tank

KV-1 tank

KV-1 Tank

Weight	43 tons
Crew	Five
Armament	76.2mm gun and three 7.62mm DT machine-guns
Armour	Max: 75mm. Min: 35mm
Engine	V-2K V-12, 550hp, speed 22mph
Dimensions	Length: 22ft 3in. Width: 10ft 11in. Height: 10ft 8in
Production	10,000

IS-2 'Stalin' Tank

Weight	45.5 tons
Crew	Four
Armament	122mm gun and three 7.62mm DT machine-guns
Armour	Max: 120mm. Min: 14mm
Engine	V-2 V-12, 513hp, speed 23mph
Dimensions	Length: 32ft 2in. Width: 10ft Height: 8ft 11in
Production	2,350

IS-2 'Stalin' tank

T-34/76 tank in combat

Soviet Aircraft

When the Germans invaded the USSR in June 1941 the majority of the first-line aircraft of the Soviet Air Force were, by German standards, obsolete. The principal fighter was the Polikarpov I-16, which was, however, woefully inferior to the Bf 109. Soviet bombers, with their meagre bomb capacity, were equally ineffective.

Gradually, better types, such as the LaGG-3 and the Yak-1 fighters, began to replace the huge numbers that had been lost in the early part of the German invasion. The Yak-1/3/7/9 family of fighters did more than any other group of aircraft in bringing about the defeat of the Luftwaffe, along with the superb Lavochkin La-5 and La-7.

The highly effective Il-2 Shturmovik ground-attack plane began to enter service in the winter of 1941–42. This heavily armoured aircraft proved particularly difficult to shoot down. Then came the formidable and very versa-tile Petlyakov Pe-2 bomber, which was the Soviet counterpart to the British Mosquito but built in much greater numbers. The only effective heavy four-engined bomber produced by the Soviets was the Petlyakov Pe-8, but only 81 were built as Soviet efforts were concentrated on tactical air operations.

Slowly the Soviet Air Force's capability began to match that of the Luftwaffe and was then able to defeat it.

Yak-3

Yakovlev Yak-3

Weight	5,864lb
Crew	One
Armament	One 20mm cannon and two 12.7mm machine-guns
Range	560 miles
Engine	Klimov, 1,300hp, max. speed 407mph
Dimensions	Length: 27ft 10in. Wing span: 30ft 2in. Height: 7ft 11in
Production	4,848

Il-2 Shturmovik

Ilyushin Il-2 Shturmovik

Weight	14,000lb
Crew	Two
Armament	Two 23mm cannon, two 7.62mm machine-guns and one 12.7mm machine-gun, plus 1,321lb bomb-load
Range	475 miles
Engine	Mikulin, 1,770hp, max. speed 251mph
Dimensions	Length: 38ft 0in. Wing span: 47ft 11in. Height: 11ft 2in
Production	36,150

Petlyakov Pe-2

Weight	18,730lb
Crew	Three–four
Armament	Three 7.62 or 12.7mm machine-guns, 2,645lb bomb-load
Range	930 miles
Engine	Two Klimov, 1,100hp, max. speed 336mph
Dimensions	Length: 41ft 6in. Wing span: 56ft 3in. Height: 13ft 1in
Production	11,427 (all marks)

Petlyakov Pe-2 bomber

The Polish Army on September 1, 1939 was less than 300,000 strong, though it had a large number of reservists. It was made up of 30 infantry divisions and 11 cavalry divisions, but only two mechanised brigades. Polish cavalry units were only just beginning to be mechanised. The Germans, on the other hand, had more than 100 divisions, including five powerful Panzer divisions and eight mechanised or motorised divisions, totalling some 2.5 million well-trained soldiers.

The Polish Air Force had only 154 bombers and 159 fighters but, apart from some bombers, these were mostly obsolescent aircraft. The Germans had over four times that number and all modern, state-of-the-art warplanes.

The Poles fought bravely, but bravery is often not enough. They quickly succumbed to the better-equipped and far more numerous foe. Moreover, the Germans had a much better appreciation of modern, fast-moving, mechanised warfare.

Seventeen days after the campaign began Soviet troops also invaded

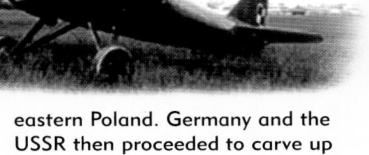

PZL P.11 fighter

eastern Poland. Germany and the USSR then proceeded to carve up Poland between them once organised Polish resistance had ended on October 6, 1939.

Some 100,000 Polish soldiers would escape and form the Free Polish Brigade in France and then England, where they would continue to fight the Nazis on land, sea and in the air.

Polish light tanks, the 7 TP

Polish cavalry

Norway and Denmark

On April 9, 1940, when the Germans invaded, Denmark's small army was a meagre 14,000 strong and her tiny Navy consisted of two small coastal defence vessels. Her Naval/Army Air Force consisted of just 50 aircraft, mostly obsolete. The Germans were offered only token resistance by the Danes, who suffered 26 dead. The invasion was a total success for the Germans.

The Norwegians, who had enjoyed over 100 years of uninterrupted peace, could only field an army of about 100,000 men, but they still put up a stubborn defence against the German invaders. Norway did not have any tank units, because of the very mountainous terrain, and relied on infantry and artillery.

Norway's tiny navy also gave a very good account of itself despite the fact that most of its vessels were obsolete. The Norwegian merchant fleet, totalling four million tons (and 1,000 ships), had been requisitioned by the Norwegian government in April 1940. Because this government was in exile,

residing in Britain, these ships went on to play an indispensable part in the Allied cause during the Battle of the Atlantic.

A large part of the Norwegian Air Force was equipped with the semi-modern Gloster Gladiator fighter, but with just 76 aircraft there was little

Danish artillery

that could be done, especially as the Luftwaffe had all but destroyed them on the opening day of the fighting.

After two months of heavy fighting, and despite the aid of British, French and Free Polish forces, Norway capitulated on June 9, 1940.

Norwegian soldiers

During World War I the neutrality of the Netherlands had been respected, but in April 1940 the Dutch armed forces mobilised because of the strong possibility that this time it would not be. Certain German officers who had misgivings about invading the neutral Netherlands warned the Dutch of the exact date of the forthcoming invasion – May 10, 1940.

The Dutch field army when fully mobilised was made up of eight divisions and eight brigades and numbered 270,000 including reservists. Because of a strong Dutch pacifist movement within the country, the Army was not allowed to modernise or train properly. It did not possess a single tank and only a few armoured cars. The artillery was made up of totally outdated guns. Unsurprisingly, despite many valiant acts of bravery, the Army was incapable of resisting the Germans.

The Dutch Air Force did not fare any better. It had just 175 aircraft, of which only 72 were modern. It was opposed by 1,100 modern German aircraft.

The small but modern Navy was primarily employed to defend the Dutch East Indies, which it did until 1942, when it was annihilated by the Japanese.

One of the few Belgian tanks

After the heavy bombing and the destruction of the centre of Rotterdam by the Luftwaffe, the Dutch government felt compelled to capitulate. The invasion and conquest of the Netherlands had taken just five days.

In May 1940 the Belgian Army had 22 divisions of 550,000 troops. Unfortunately it possessed only ten tanks and few anti-aircraft guns.

Of the 250 aircraft at its disposal, only 50 could be considered modern.

The tenacity of Belgian soldiers surprised the Germans, but after 18 days of very bitter fighting the King decided to surrender in the face of total German military superiority.

Dutch artillery

Greece and Yugoslavia

The Greek armed forces suffered from a shortage of modern weapons. When the Italians invaded in October 1940 the Army totalled 18 divisions and numbered 430,000 men. The mountainous terrain along the Greek/Albanian frontier was well suited to the Greek defence, and the outnumbered Greeks were able to contain the invading Italian forces and then force them back into Albania from where they came.

Yugoslavian troops

With only 120 aircraft, the outnumbered Greek Air Force put up a brave and stubborn resistance against overwhelming numbers of Italian aircraft. By the time of the German invasion in April 1941 only 41 Greek aircraft were operational.

Less than six months later the Greek Army and British forces sent to aid them were totally overwhelmed by the Germans on April 6, 1941. The country capitulated on April 20.

The Yugoslavian Army, including reserves, had a strength on paper of nearly 1,200,000 troops. It had only 110 obsolescent light tanks and the Army moved at a walking pace. When the German attack came on April 6, 1941 the front crumbled, and when the Italian and Hungarian forces joined the assault two days later any organised resistance quickly began to fail; by April 17 it had totally collapsed.

The Yugoslavian Air Force had approximately 500 aircraft, but when pitted against the might of the Luftwaffe it stood little chance and by the end of the first week of fighting had almost ceased to exist.

The invasion of the Balkans forced Hitler to postpone his invasion of Russia by six vital weeks and the German Army was anxious to redeploy in preparation for that task. Therefore, the task of rounding up and disarming defeated Yugoslavian soldiers was not carried out effectively and perhaps as many as 300,000 managed to retain their arms. Many of these joined the resistance under such leaders as Tito and fought on in the mountains.

Greek machine-gunners

Chinese Armed Forces

4

The Nationalist and Communist Chinese forces, sworn enemies, nevertheless agreed a rapprochement in order to face the common foe, the Japanese.

The Nationalist Chinese forces, led by Chiang Kai-shek, had about 1,500,000 men in 1937 when the Japanese invaded China. During the first year they lost nearly 1 million men to the Japanese. The remainder of them traded space for time as the Japanese advanced into central and southern China. These advances slowed and came to a stop as a war of attrition developed. As the Japanese slowly began to cut off access to the rest of the world, Nationalists eventually became reliant on only one supply route, the Burma Road, to bring in military aid. Their army was short of such items as tanks and medium and heavy artillery and their air force had been all but destroyed by mid-1938. By 1940 the American General Chennault established his 'Flying Tigers' to aid the Nationalists. These US volunteer pilots and P-40 aircraft never numbered

more than 200 aircraft. By the war's end the Nationalists had some 300 divisions each with a strength of some 10,000.

The Communists of Mao Tse-tung were the Japanese forces' main opponents in the north of China. Within a few months of the start of hostilities the Communists had three divisions established behind enemy lines. Initial losses were heavy, especially during the 'Hundred Regiments' Campaign' of 1940. In 1937 they had 90,000 troops but by 1945 they had some 900,000, with local militia units as well as regular units.

Altogether Chinese military casualties numbered over 1,300,000 killed and 1,750,000 wounded during the eight years of combat.

Chinese Communist troops with captured Japanese tanks

A P-40 Hawk of the 'Flying Tigers'

ARMED FORCES China

Poland/The Campaign in the West

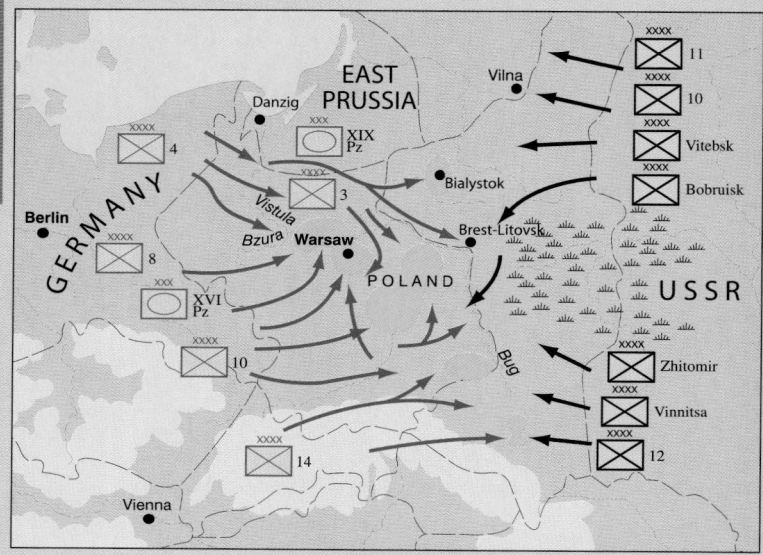

POLAND

German troops cross the frontier into Poland, September 1, 1939.

Britain and France declare war on Germany, September 3.

Battle of the River Bzura, Polish Poznan Army tries to avoid encirclement, September 12.

Warsaw surrounded by German forces, September 15.

Soviet forces invade Poland, September 17.

Polish Poznan Army surrenders, the Germans taking 170,000 prisoners, September 18.

Soviet and German troops meet at Brest-Litovsk, September 19.

Warsaw surrenders to Germans, September 22.

Ten Polish Divisions surrender in the Modlin area, September 28.

Polish resistance ends, October 6.

POLAND: LOSSES

	GERMANY	POLAND
Killed	8,000	70,000
Wounded	27,300	130,000

THE CAMPAIGN IN THE WEST

Germans invade Belgium and the Netherlands, May 10, 1940.

Allies enter Belgium to take up positions to oppose the Germans, May 10, 1940.

The Netherlands surrenders, May 15.

Allies withdraw from Belgium, May 16.

Germans enter Brussels, May 17.

German Panzer forces reach the Channel at the mouth of the River Somme, splitting the Allied armies in two, May 20.

British counter-attack at Arras fails, May 21.

'Operation Dynamo', evacuation of British, French and Belgian troops

POLAND: OPPOSING FORCES

	GERMANY	POLAND
Infantry Divisions	40	30
Tank Divisions	11	1 brigade
Bomber Aircraft	850	210
Fighter Aircraft	400	150

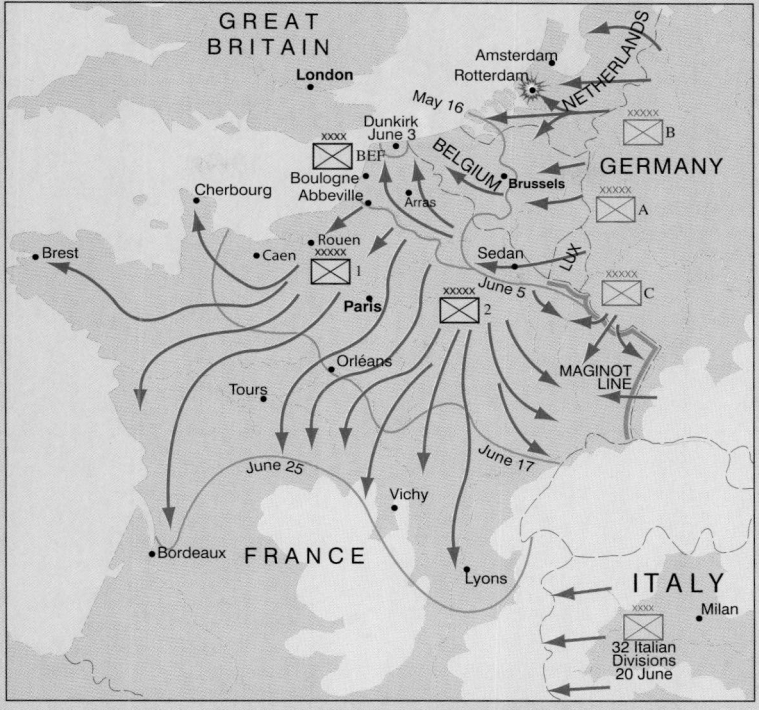

THE WEST: OPPOSING FORCES				
Forces	**GERMANY**	**FRANCE**	**BRITAIN**	**BELGIUM**	**NETHERLANDS**
Divisions	141	104	10	22	8
Tanks	2,445	3,063	310	10	1
Aircraft	4,020	1,368	456	250	175

from Dunkirk, May 26.
Belgium surrenders, May 27.
Main German offensive switches south, May 29.
French forces routed on the River Somme, June 9.

Italy declares war on Britain and France June 11.
Germans enter Paris, June 14.
Italy invades France, June 20.
France signs armistice with Germany, June 22.

THE WEST: LOSSES					
	GERMANY	**FRANCE**	**BELGIUM**	**NETHERLANDS**	**BRITAIN**
Killed	29,600	90,000	6,000	2,100	3,500
Wounded	133,600	200,000	15,900	2,700	15,800
Prisoner	—	1,900,000	200,000	—	40,000

GERMAN, ITALIAN & BRITISH FORCES			
	GERMANY	ITALY	BRITAIN
Divs	33	28	4

BALKAN ARMED FORCES					
Forces	BULGARIA	HUNGARY	ROMANIA	YUGOSLAVIA	GREECE
Troops	650,000	700,000	1,700,000	1,400,000	500,000
Aircraft	100	1,000	1,000	800	120

Axis forces invade Yugoslavia and Greece, April 6, 1941.

Salonika captured by Germans, April 9.

British troops begin to retreat from northern Greece, April 10.

Belgrade occupied by Germans, April 13.

Sarajevo occupied, April 16.

Yugoslavia surrenders to the Axis, April 17.

Greek First Army surrenders, April 20.

British forces begin their evacuation of Greece, April 22.

German troops capture Athens, April 27.

British forces complete their evacuation to Crete, April 28.

German airborne troops begin attack on Crete, May 20.

Allied evacuation of Crete starts May 28 and is completed by June 1.

North Africa and the Mediterranean

British capture Forts Capuzzo and Maddalena in Libya, June 14, 1940.

Inconclusive naval battle off Calabria between Italian and British fleets, July 9.

Italians invade Egypt but advance only 60 miles, September 16.

Taranto attacked by Royal Navy torpedo bombers, November 11.

Allies counter-attack, December 9.

Tobruk captured by Australian troops, January 22, 1941.

Benghazi captured by Australian troops, February 6.

Battle of Beda Fomm, British victory, February 6–7.

El Agheila captured by British, February 9.

Battle of Cape Matapan, British naval victory, March 28/29.

Germans defeat British in tank battle at Mersa Brega, 24 March

Germans take Benghazi, April 4.

Tobruk besieged by Axis, April 11.

British retreat from Halfaya Pass, April 25.

British tank reinforcements arrive at Alexandria, May 12.

Operation 'Battleaxe' to relieve the siege of Tobruk fails, June 15.

Operation 'Crusader' Eighth Army offensive relieves Tobruk, December 7.

Eighth Army forces Rommel to retreat to El Agheila, January 6, 1942.

Rommel counter-attacks, retaking Benghazi, January 29.

Axis advance stops on the Gazala/Bir Hacheim defences, February 4.

Rommel wins the Battle of Gazala, June 18.

Tobruk captured by the Axis, 21 June.

Rommel advances to Mersa Matruh, June 29.

Eighth Army falls back to El Alamein defensive positions, June 30.

ITALIAN & BRITISH FORCES, DECEMBER 1940

	ITALY	BRITISH
Divisions	5	3

AXIS & EIGHTH ARMY, BATTLE OF GAZALA, JUNE 1942

GERMANS/ITALIANS	EIGHTH ARMY
90,000 men 560 tanks (332 German 228 Italian) 700 aircraft (310 German 390 Italian)	100,000 men 849 tanks 320 aircraft

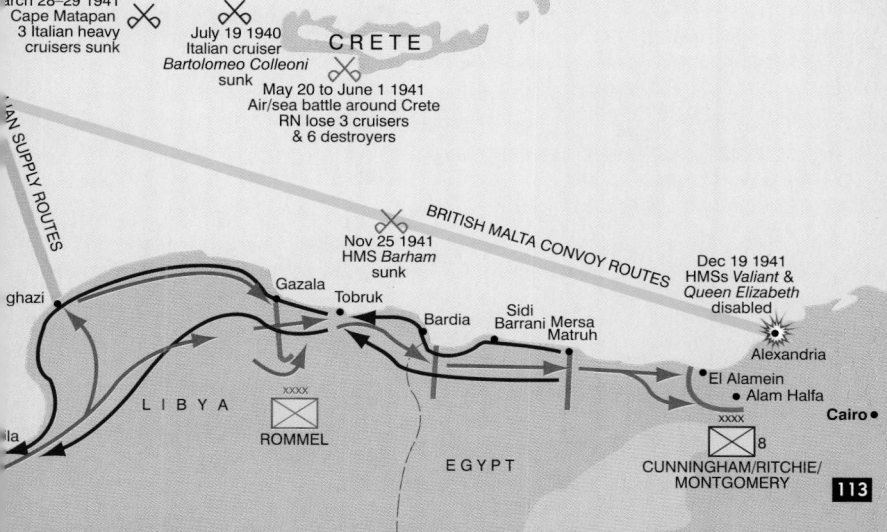

'Barbarossa': Invasion of Russia

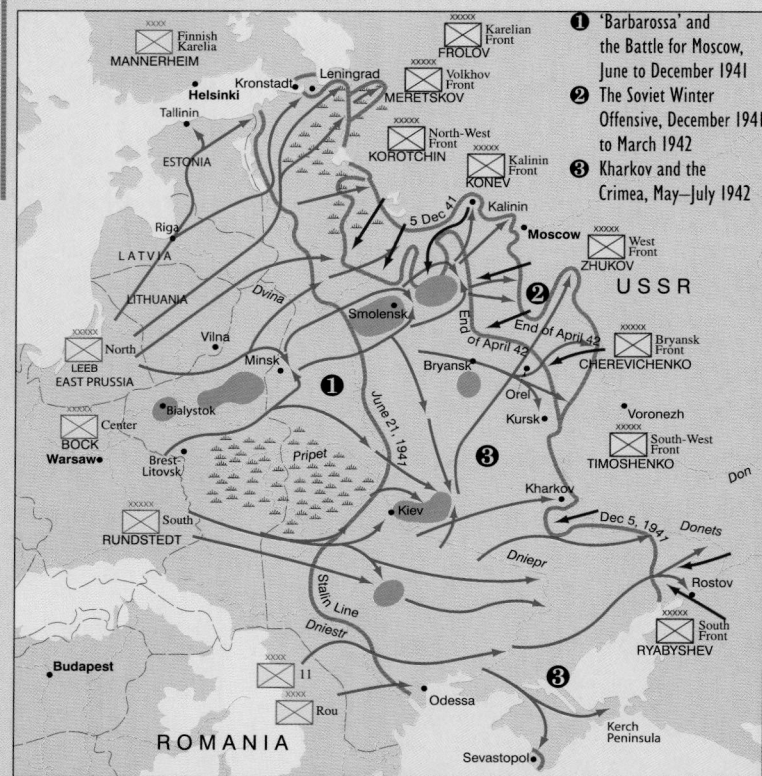

❶ 'Barbarossa' and the Battle for Moscow, June to December 1941

❷ The Soviet Winter Offensive, December 1941 to March 1942

❸ Kharkov and the Crimea, May–July 1942

Operation 'Barbarossa', the invasion of the Soviet Union, June 22, 1941.

290,000 Soviet troops surrender in Bialystok pocket, June 30.

300,000 Soviet troops captured in the Smolensk pocket, August 5.

100,000 Soviet troops taken in Uman pocket, August 8.

Leningrad besieged, September 4.

Germans capture Kiev, 600,000 Soviet prisoners taken, September 19.

German drive to Moscow begins, September 30.

Bryansk pocket surrenders, 50,000 Soviet prisoners taken, October 14.

670,000 Soviet troops surrender in Vyazma pocket, October 19.

Kursk captured by Germans, November 3.

'BARBAROSSA': FORCES

	GERMANY/AXIS	USSR
Troops	3,600,000	2,900,000
Divisions	153	140
Tanks	3,600	10–15,000
Aircraft	2,700	8,000

German advance halts 19 miles from centre of Moscow, December 5.

Major Soviet counter-attack defending Moscow, December 5.

Soviet counter-offensive halts, but it has denied the Germans Moscow, March 19, 1942.

German offensive south of Kharkov, May 18.

Crimea taken by the Germans, July 3.

Pearl Harbor and the Philippines

Pearl Harbor attacked by Japanese Navy aircraft (two US battleships are total losses, four sink in the shallow water of the harbour and are repairable) December 7, 1941.

Tarawa and Makin Islands captured by Japanese, December 9.

Japanese invade Borneo, December 16.

Japanese land on Luzon in Philippines, December 22.

Japanese capture Wake Island from US garrison, December 23.

Japanese land near Manila, December 24.

Japanese enter Manila, January 2, 1942

US and Filipino forces withdraw to the Bataan peninsula, January 5.

Japanese land at Rabaul, New Ireland, January 23.

Darwin, Northern Australia, raided by Japanese aircraft, which cause extensive damage, February 19.

Japanese naval victory at Battle of Java Sea, February 27.

Japanese naval victory at Battle of Sunda Strait, March 1.

Dutch Government flees Java, March 7.

78,000 Allies surrender on the Bataan peninsula, April 9.

Japanese take Cebu Islands, April 10.

The fortress island of Corregidor surrenders, May 5.

Philippine Islands surrender to the Japanese, May 10.

JAPANESE NAVY: DECEMBER 1941		
	IN SERVICE	BUILDING
Battleships	10	2
Carriers	10	4
Heavy cruisers	18	—
Light cruisers	20	4
Destroyers	112	12
Submarines	65	29

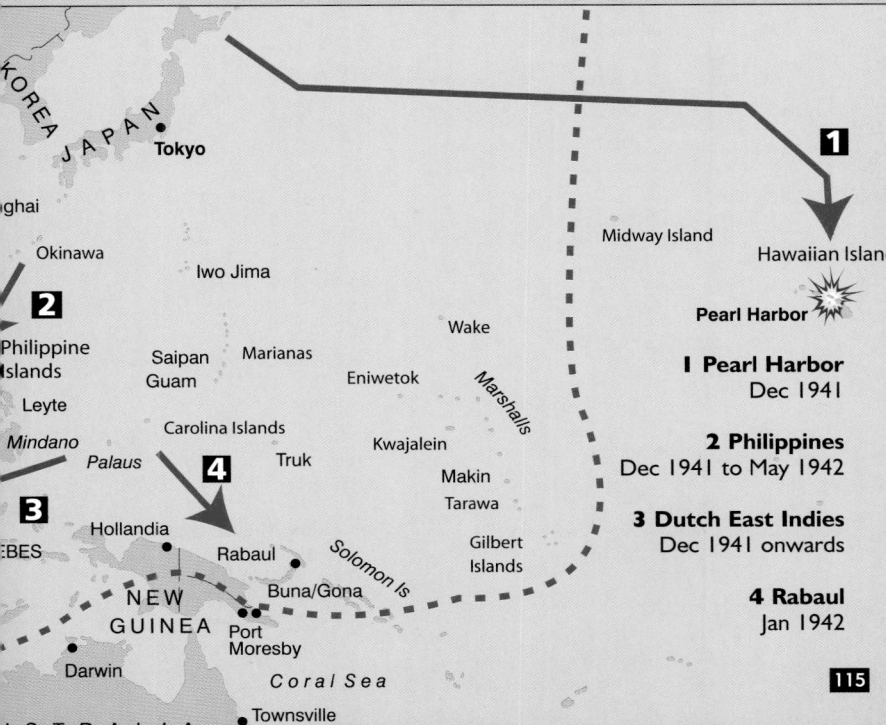

1 Pearl Harbor
Dec 1941

2 Philippines
Dec 1941 to May 1942

3 Dutch East Indies
Dec 1941 onwards

4 Rabaul
Jan 1942

Malaya, Singapore and Burma

1 Dec 1941
2 Dec 1941 to Feb 1942
3 Dec 1941 onwards
4 Dec 1941 to May 1942

Ceylon bombed by Japanese carrier aircraft, April 5.

Two British cruisers sunk in Indian Ocean by Japanese carrier aircraft, April 5.

British carrier sunk by carrier aircraft, April 9.

Mandalay captured by Japanese, May 1.

Japanese conquer Burma, May 20.

DEFEAT

The fall of Singapore was, in the words of Winston Churchill, 'the worst disaster and largest capitulation in British history'.

The fall of the Philippines was the worst defeat suffered by American arms since the War of 1812.

Vichy French Indo-China allows Japanese troops into the country, July 23, 1941.

Singapore bombed by Japanese aircraft, December 8.

Japanese invade Malaya, December 8

Two British battleships sunk by Japanese aircraft, December 10.

Thailand allied with Japan, December 14.

Point Victoria in southern Burma seized by Japanese, December 15.

Rangoon bombed by Japanese aircraft, December 23.

Hong Kong captured by the Japanese, December 25.

Burma invaded by Japanese, January 20.

British troops abandon Malaya and retire to the island of Singapore, January 31.

Singapore surrenders to Japanese, February 15.

Rangoon taken by Japanese, March 8.

Japanese occupy Andaman Islands, March 23.

Mandalay heavily bombed by Japanese, April 3.

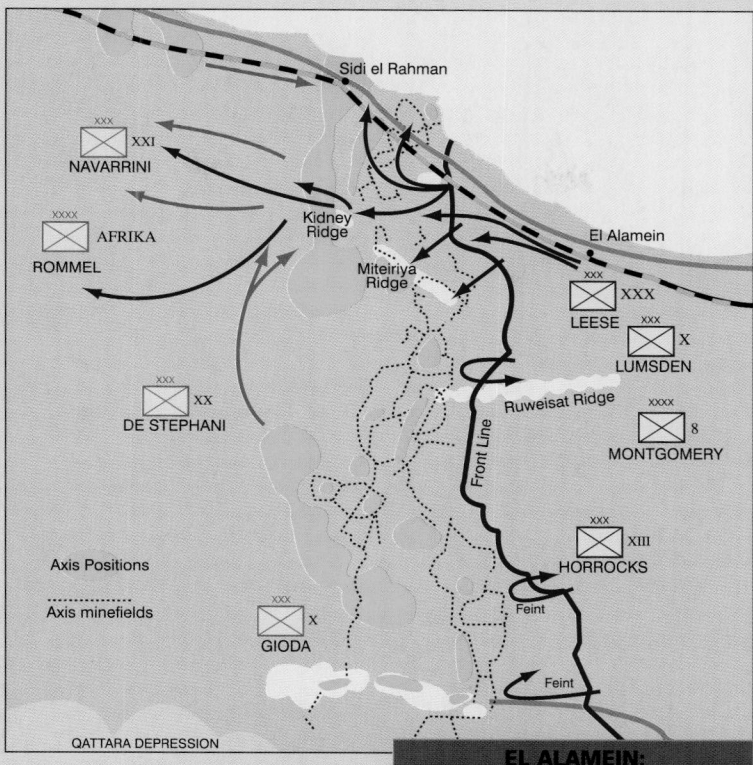

Rommel begins attacks on British positions, July 1, 1942.

Rommel stopped by Eighth Army, July 27.

Montgomery takes command of Eighth Army, August 13.

Rommel again halted at Battle of Alam Halfa, September 2.

Battle of El Alamein starts, October 23.

Axis counter-attack repulsed, October 27.

Rommel withdraws his troops, November 2.

Tobruk recaptured by Eighth Army, November 13

Benghazi taken by Allies, November 20.

Axis forces halt at El Agheila, November 24.

Axis forces resume retreat from El Agheila, December 13.

Rommel halts retreat at Buerat, December 23.

Rommel resumes retreat from Buerat, January 13, 1943.

Axis forces retreat into Tunisia, January 23.

Eighth Army takes Tripoli, January 23.

	EL ALAMEIN: OPPOSING FORCES	
	AXIS	**BRITAIN/ DOMINION**
Troops	50,000 Germans 54,000 Italians	195,000
Tanks	496	1,029
Aircraft	350	530

5 Midway and Guadalcanal

Dutch Harbor in the Aleutians attacked by Japanese carrier planes, June 4, 1942.

Battle of Midway, Japanese lose three carriers, major US victory, June 4.

Japanese lose another carrier, June 5.

US Navy loses a carrier, June, 7.

Japanese land on Aleutian Islands of Attu and Kiska, June 7.

US landing on Solomon island of Guadalcanal seizing a Japanese airfield and naming it Henderson Field, August 7.

Battle of Savo Island, four US cruisers sunk, August 8.

Japanese troops repulsed on Gaudalcanal, August 21.

Battle of Solomon Islands, Japanese carrier sunk, August 23–25.

Battle of Bloody Ridge, Guadalcanal, Japanese repulsed, September 12–14.

US carrier sunk by a Japanese submarine, September 15.

Battle of Cape Esperance, US loses a cruiser, as do the Japanese, October 11/12.

Battle for Henderson Field, Japanese defeated, October 23–26.

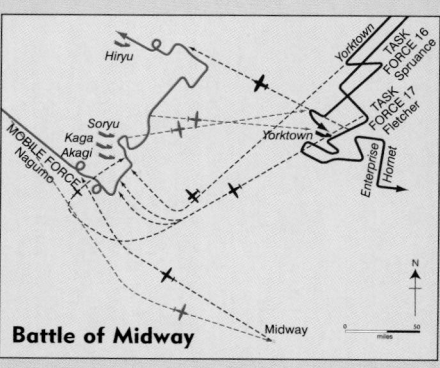

Battle of Midway

Battle of Santa Cruz Island, US loses a carrier but the Japanese lose more aircraft and have a carrier badly damaged, October 26/7.

First Naval Battle of Guadalcanal, US loses two cruisers, the Japanese two battleships and a cruiser, November 12/13.

Second Naval Battle of Guadalcanal, Japanese lose a battleship, November 14/15.

Battle of Tassafaronga, US tactical success, November 30.

US troops push westwards, December –January 1943.

Guadalcanal secured by US forces as Japanese evacuate island after six months of bitter fighting, February 9.

FORCES ON GUADALCANAL

	USA	JAPAN
Aug 7	10,000	2,200
Sept 11	11,000	9,000
Nov 12	29,000	30,000
Dec 1	40,000	25,000

Caucasus to Stalingrad

5

CAMPAIGNS

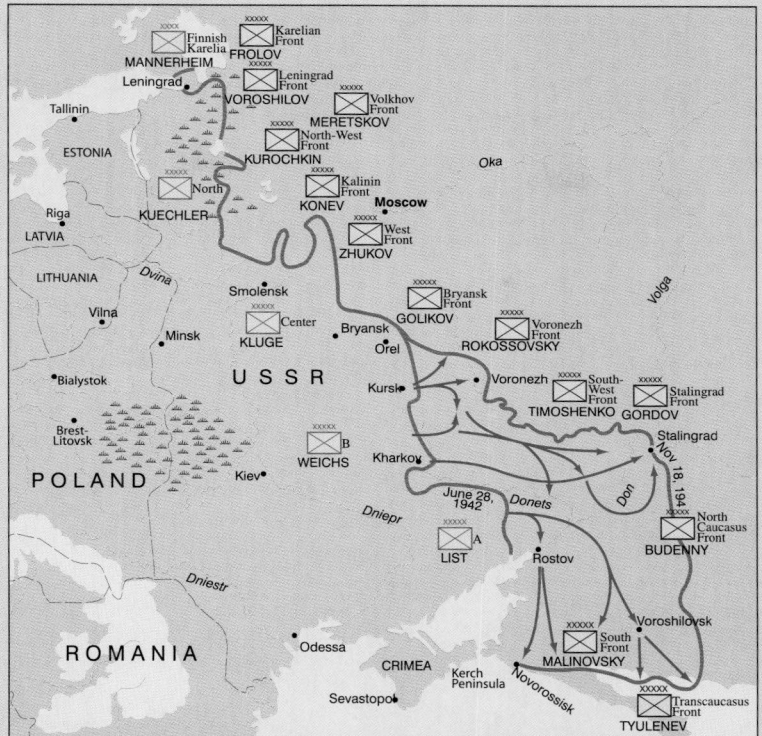

German Army Group A attacks into the River Donets basin, July 7, 1942.

Army Group B advances towards Stalingrad, July 18.

Army Group A crosses the River Don, July 25.

German Sixth Army reaches the outskirts of Stalingrad, August 10.

German Sixth Army attacks Stalingrad, August 19.

Army Group A reaches the Caucasus Mountains, August 23.

Soviet troops defend Stalingrad desperately, September–October.

Soviet counter-attack begins, November 19.

Soviet troops from the south-west and to the north link up and German

Sixth Army is now trapped, November 23.

Göring declares that the Luftwaffe can supply the Sixth Army by air, November 24.

Operation 'Winter Storm', von Manstein's unsuccessful attempt to relieve the Germans under siege, is lauched, December 12.

Soviets re-open the offensive as they squeeze the German pocket, January 10, 1943.

Last German airfield falls to the Soviets, January 21.

The Soviet final assault begins, January 22.

Hitler forbids break-out, January 24.

German Sixth Army surrenders, January 31.

Convoy War: Atlantic and Arctic

British liner *Athenia* sunk by U-boat, September 3, 1939.

Aircraft carrier HMS *Courageous* sunk by U-boat, September 17.

Battleship HMS *Royal Oak* sunk by U-boat at its base, Scapa Flow, October 14.

German pocket battleship *Admiral Graf Spee* scuttled after Battle of River Plate, December 17.

By the end of 1939 German surface ships had sunk 15 vessels, U-boats 114, mines 79.

U-boat 'wolfpacks' begin to operate, June 1940.

8 U-boats attack British convoy sinking 32 ships, October 17–20, 1940.

During 1940 Germans sink 511 Allied ships.

Battlecruiser HMS *Hood* sunk by *Bismarck*, May 24, 1941.

Bismarck sunk by British warships, May 27.

During 1941 Germans sink 568 Allied ships.

During 1942 Germans sink 590 Allied ships.

In US waters 65 merchant vessels lost to U-boats in February, 1942.

Convoy PQ17 loses 24 vessels of the 34 that set sail for Russia, July.

41 U-boats sunk during May 1943, Allies gaining the ascendancy.

German battleship *Scharnhorst* sunk by British warships, North Cape, December 26.

In 1943 Germans sink 203 Allied ships.

German battleship *Tirpitz* sunk by RAF bombers, Norway, November 12, 1944.

By the end of 1944 Germans have sunk 102 Allied ships.

By May 1945 Germans have sunk 45 Allied ships.

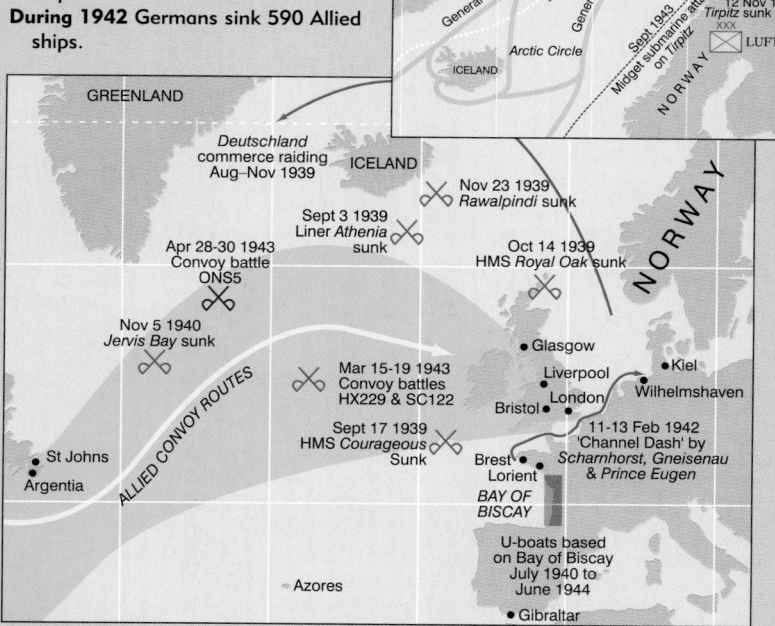

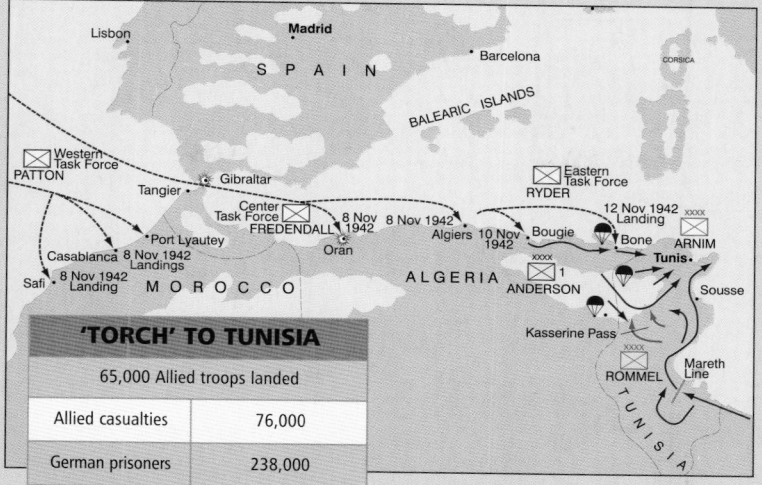

'TORCH' TO TUNISIA	
65,000 Allied troops landed	
Allied casualties	76,000
German prisoners	238,000

Operation 'Torch', Allied amphibious landings in Morocco and Algeria, November 8, 1942.

Vichy French resistance ceases, November 10.

Allied forces invade Tunisia from Algeria, November 15.

Vichy French forces in Tunisia join with the Allies in fighting the Axis, November 18.

Allies halt advance into Tunisia running short of supplies, November 21.

Allies renew their advance on Tunis, November 24.

Vichy French Fleet scuttled at Toulon to avoid being taken by the Germans, November 27.

10th Panzer Division forces Allies to withdraw from their attempt to take Tunis, December 1.

Battle of Longstop Hill, Allies repulsed, December 22–25.

Allies pause before continuing their offensive against Tunis, December 28.

Successful offensive, Operation 'Eilbote', by Axis commanded by von Arnim makes gains against French and US forces, January 18, 1943.

Montgomery's Eighth Army advances into Tunisia, February 7

Further German gains, February 14–18.

Battle of Kasserine Pass, Rommel defeats US armoured forces, February 19.

Kasserine Pass is retaken by the Allies, February 25.

Patton with II Corps begins advance further into Tunisia, February 25.

Battle of Medenine, Eighth Army repulses offensive by Rommel, March 6.

Battle for the Mareth Line, Eighth Army breaks through, March 20–30.

Patton's advance is halted at Fondouk and Faid, March 31.

Eighth Army advances to Enfidaville 40 miles from Tunis, 150 miles in one month, April 21.

Allies', First Army begins offensive against Tunis, 22 April.

Tunis and Bizerta captured by the Allies, May 7.

Axis resistance finally ceases in Tunis, May 11.

Papua/New Guinea

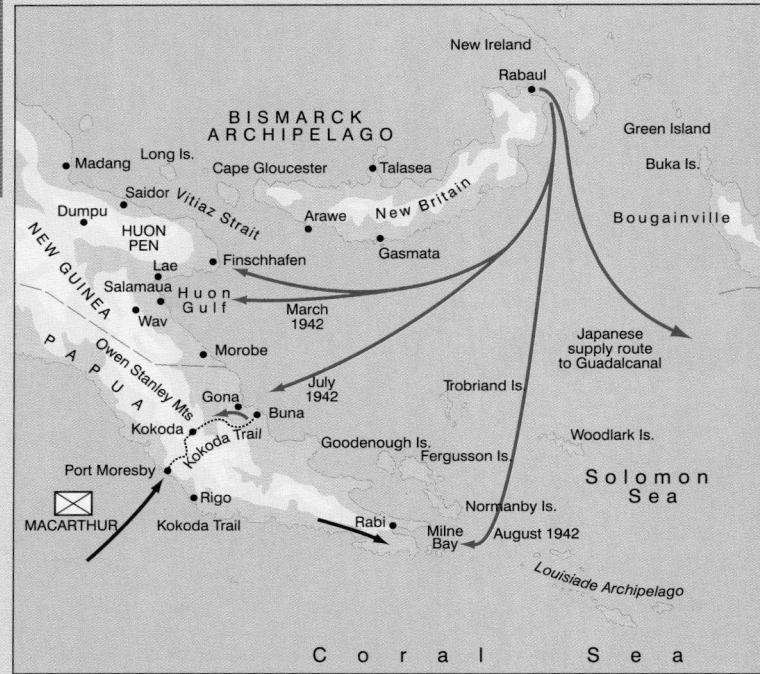

Battle of the Coral Sea, first carrier-versus-carrier battle, Japanese sink one US carrier and US sink one Japanese carrier, May 8, 1942.

Australian and Papuan forces advance to Kokoda along the Kokoda Trail, July 15.

Japanese forces at Gona, July 21.

First clashes between Japanese and Australian/Papuan forces, Japanese take Kokoda, July 23.

Kokoda is retaken by Australians and Papuans, who are, however, forced to evacuate once more, August 8.

Two brigades of Australian troops land at Port Moresby, August 8.

Main Japanese force lands at Buna, August 18.

Japanese forces land at Milne Bay, August 26.

Australians counter-attack at Milne Bay, August 28.

Japanese expelled from Milne Bay, September 6.

Japanese halt Australian attempt to recover Kokoda, September 14.

US troops land at Port Moresby, September 15.

Australians again advance along Kokoda trail, September 27.

US troops advance, October 6.

Battle of Eora Creek, Australians push through, October 21–28.

Battle of Oivi, again Australians prevail, October 5–10.

Americans and Australians continue their advance, November 14.

Japanese land reinforcements from Rabaul, December 2.

Australians take Gona, December 10.

Buna captured by Allies, January 2, 1943.

Japanese resistance in Papua ends, January 22.

Sicily and Italy

Allies invade Sicily, July 10, 1943.

Montgomery takes the Primasole Bridge and advances north towards Messina, July 13.

Patton advances to the north-west towards Palermo, July 16.

US troops take Enna, July 20.

US troops enter Palermo, July 23.

British forces take Catania, August 5.

Germans evacuate Sicily, August 12.

US forces advance along the north coast of Sicily and take Messina, August 17.

British land in Calabria, Italy, where opposition is light, September 3.

Allies land at Salerno in Italy, September 9.

German counter-attack at Salerno thwarted, September 14.

German troops slowly begin to withdraw northwards, September 16.

US Fifth Army enters Naples, October 1.

British Eighth Army attacks the Gustav Line, November 20.

Allies land at Anzio, January 22, 1944.

Allies bomb the monastery at Monte Cassino, February 15.

Germans counter-attack the Anzio beachhead, February 16.

Monte Cassino is finally taken after four months of costly battles, May 17.

US Fifth Army enters Rome, June 5.

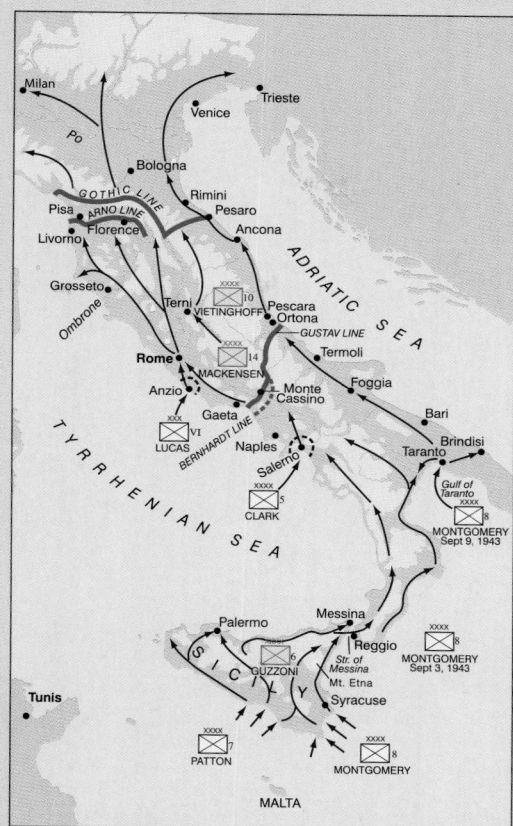

British V Corps and Canadian I Corps attack the Gothic Line, August 30.

US Fifth Army begins its next offensive, September 12.

US troops advance to Bologna, September 24

British Eighth Army advances north to the River Rubicon, October 12.

German counter-attack stopped in the Serchio valley, December 26.

US troops take Parma and Verona, April 25, 1945.

US troops reach Genoa, April 27.

Italian partisans take Milan, April 29.

British troops reach Venice, April 29.

Germans surrender, April 29.

Central Pacific

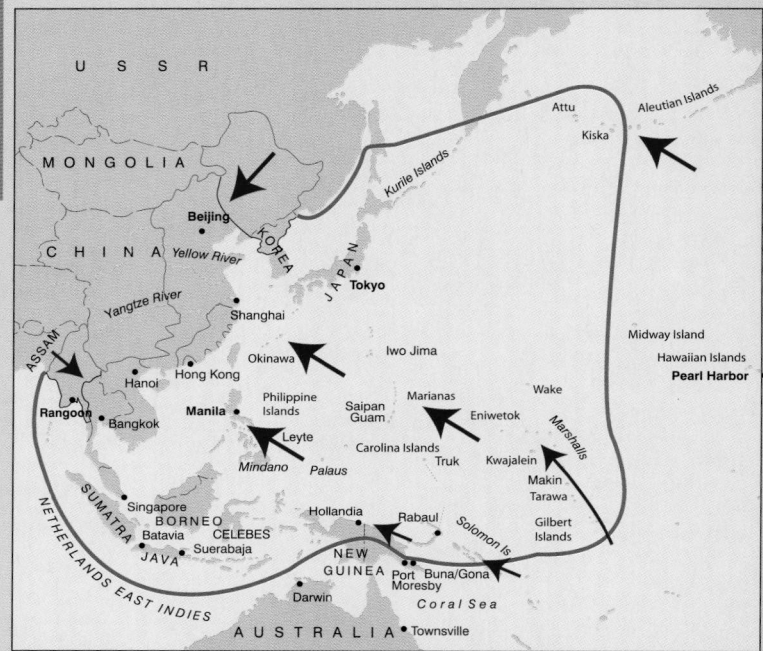

US troops occupy Amchitka in the Aleutian Islands, January 12, 1943.

US victory at Battle of Bismarck Sea, March 3–5.

US Marines land on New Georgia, June 21.

US and Canadian troops land on Kiska in the Aleutian Islands, August 15.

New Georgia cleared of Japanese troops, August 25.

US land on Bougainville, November 1.

US forces land at Tarawa and Makin in the Gilbert Islands, November 20.

Tarawa and Makin captured by US, November 23.

US capture Kwajalein in the Marshall Islands, February 4, 1944.

Battle of Eniwetok Atoll, US victory, February 18–23.

Rabaul isolated, US land on Emiru Island to its north, March 24.

US secure Bougainville, March 27.

US land at Hollandia, New Guinea, April 24.

At Rabaul, Japanese begin to pull out, May 14.

US naval victory at the Battle of the Philippine Sea, Japanese lose three carriers and 350 aircraft, June 19–20.

US forces land on Saipan, June 15.

US warships and aircraft bombard Guam for 13 days prior to the assault, July 8.

Saipan secured by US, July 9.

US land on Guam, July 21.

US land on Tinian, July 24.

In New Guinea, Allies secure most of the north coast and the Japanese are contained there without supplies, July 30.

Tinian secured by US, August 1.

Guam secured by US, August 10.

US forces take Peleliu and Morotai islands, September 15.

British advance down the Burmese coast into the Arakan towards Akyab, December 17, 1942.

Japanese fall back in front of the British advance, December 22.

Japanese repulse British advance at Donbaik, January 7, 1943.

Japanese repulse British advance at Akyab, February 3.

Chindits advance into Burma, February 13.

Chindits cut Mandalay/ Myitkyina railway, March 6.

British army brigade captured at Indin, April 3.

British begin to retreat almost back to their original lines, May 14.

Chindits suffer heavy losses, only two-thirds managing to return to India, April 29.

Japanese attack into the Arakan, February 3, 1944.

Chindits advance into Burma from Ledo, February 5.

Chinese forces under Stilwell defeat Japanese at Maingkwan and Walawbaum, March 6.

Japanese invasion of India begins, March 7.

Kohima besieged by Japanese, April 5.

Imphal attacked by Japanese, April 18.

Kohima relieved by British, April 21.

Japanese begin to retreat from Kohima, April 22.

Imphal and Kohima cleared of Japanese, June 22.

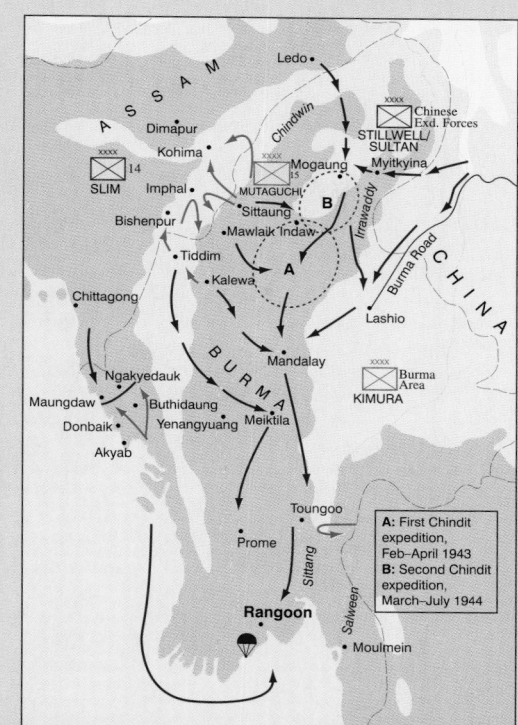

A: First Chindit expedition, Feb–April 1943
B: Second Chindit expedition, March–July 1944

Japanese retreat into Burma, July 11.

General Slim's forces advance into Burma, November 19.

British cross the Irrawaddy River and repulse Japanese counter-attack, January 16, 1945.

Meiktila falls to Indian division; Japanese counter-attack, March 3.

Mandalay taken by British, March 20.

British begin advance from Meiktila towards Rangoon, March 30.

Japanese Thirty-Third Army all but destroyed, April 6.

Japanese forces in the Arakan isolated, May 2.

Rangoon secured by British, May 3.

Japanese Taungoo offensive fails, August 4.

Japanese sign surrender in Rangoon, August 28.

Normandy

D-Day, 155,000 Allies land on the Normandy beaches, June 6, 1944.

British armoured thrust south into Normandy halted, June 14.

British and Canadians fail to take Caen, June 14.

Operation 'Epsom', British attempt to break out fails, June 30.

Cherbourg and the Carentan peninsula taken by US, June 27.

Operation 'Charnwood', attempt by the British to take Caen, only partially successful, July 11.

Seven thousand tons of bombs are dropped on Caen in an attempt to destroy the German defences, July 18.

Operation 'Goodwood', British and Canadians take Caen, July 18.

St-Lô taken by US troops, July 18.

Four thousand tons of bombs dropped on German defences prior to Operation 'Cobra', July 25.

Operation 'Cobra', US break out, Avranches taken by US troops, July 31.

Renne taken by US troops, August 3.

German counter-attack fails, August 6/7.

Patton's troops reach Lorient, August 6.

Brest reached by US troops but still holds out, August 7.

US troops take Alençon, August 8.

Operation 'Dragoon', Allies land in the south of France, August 15.

Canadians take Falaise, August 16.

Paris uprising, August 19.

Falaise Pocket closed, Allies take 50,000 German prisoners, August 21.

French and US troops enter Paris, August 25.

Toulon and Marseilles liberated by Allies, August 28.

British cross the River Somme and capture Amiens, August 31.

Brussels liberated by British, September 3.

Canadians attack Dunkirk, September 8. (But the German defenders hold out until the end of the war).

Le Havre surrenders to the

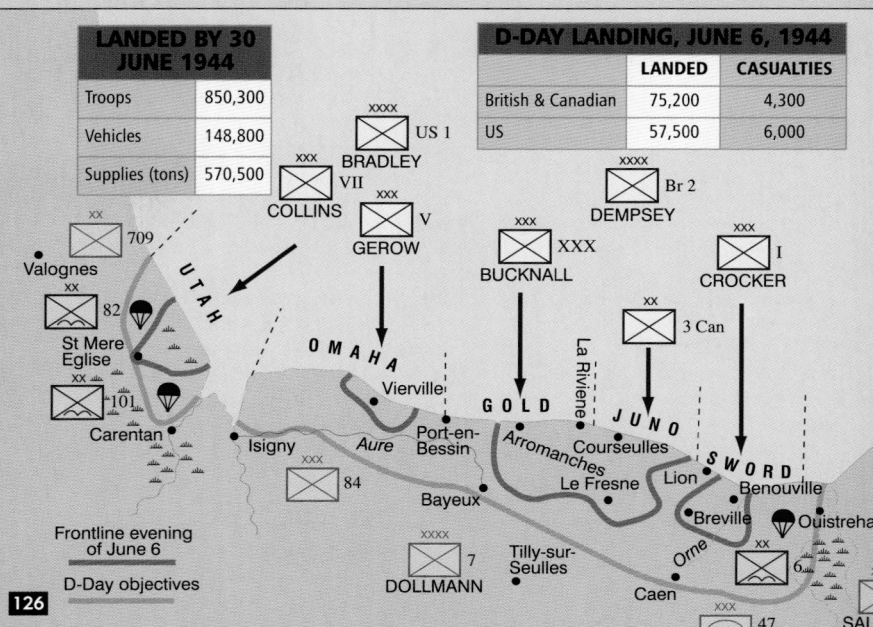

LANDED BY 30 JUNE 1944	
Troops	850,300
Vehicles	148,800
Supplies (tons)	570,500

D-DAY LANDING, JUNE 6, 1944	LANDED	CASUALTIES
British & Canadian	75,200	4,300
US	57,500	6,000

XXXX US 1
XXX BRADLEY
XXX COLLINS VII
XXX GEROW V

XXXX Br 2
DEMPSEY
XXX BUCKNALL XXX
XX 3 Can
XXX CROCKER I

XX 709
Valognes
XX 82
St Mere Eglise
XX 101
Carentan
Isigny
XXX 84
Bayeux

UTAH
OMAHA
Vierville
Aure
Port-en-Bessin
GOLD
Arromanches
La Riviere
Courseulles
Le Fresne
JUNO
Lion
Benouville
Breville
SWORD
Ouistreham

Frontline evening of June 6

D-Day objectives

XXXX 7
DOLLMANN
Tilly-sur-Seulles
Orne
Caen
XX 6
XXX 47 Pz
SAL

Liberation of France and Belgium

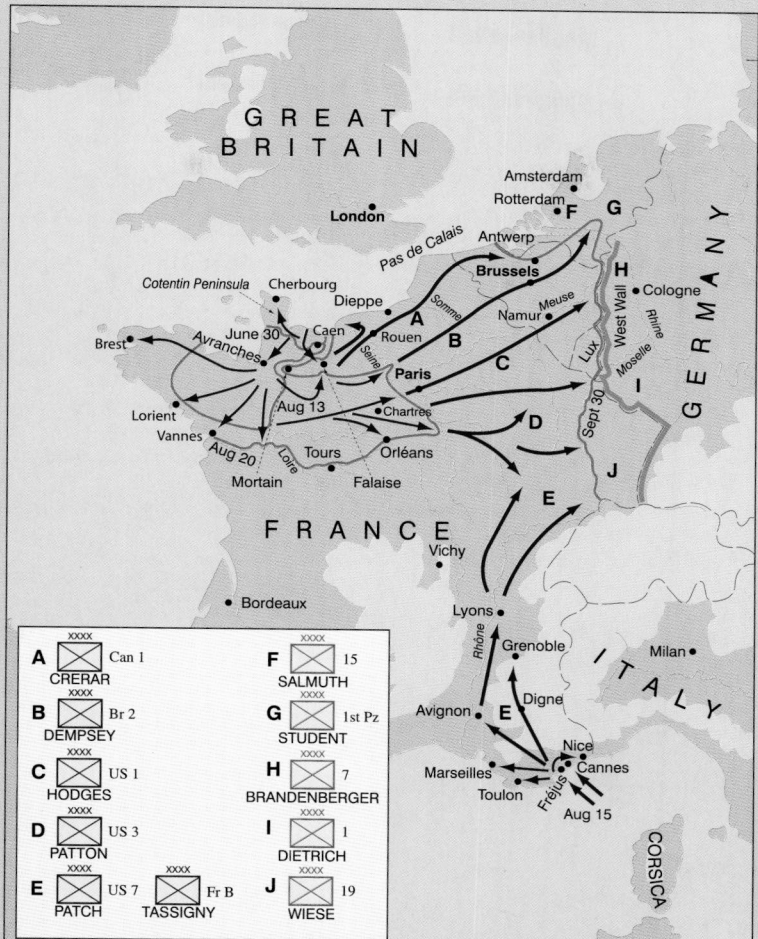

A CRERAR — Can 1
B DEMPSEY — Br 2
C HODGES — US 1
D PATTON — US 3
E PATCH — US 7   TASSIGNY — Fr B
F SALMUTH — 15
G STUDENT — 1st Pz
H BRANDENBERGER — 7
I DIETRICH — 1
J WIESE — 19

Canadians, September 12.
Brest finally falls to US troops. September 19.
Boulogne liberated by Canadians, September 22.
Operation 'Market Garden', airborne forces fail to take bridges over the Rhine, September 17–26.
Canadians clear the Scheldt estuary, making available the port of Antwerp, October 1–November 8.

Aachen falls to US troops, October 21.
US troops enter Strasbourg, November 23.
Antwerp port is now available to bring in supplies, December 1.
Patton's troops manage to break through the 'West Wall' defences, December 4.
US forces clear the west bank of the River Roer of German military units, December 9.

Stalingrad to Berlin

Germans begin to pull back from the Caucasus, January 3, 1943.

Soviet offensive across the River Don, January 13.

Soviets recapture Kursk, February 8.

Germans evacuate Kharkov, February 16.

Germans retake Kharkov, March 15.

Battle for Kursk (Operation Citadel): German offensive fails, July 13.

Russian offensive towards Kharkov, July 17.

Soviets retake Kharkov, August 23.

Soviets create bridgeheads across the Dnieper river, September 26.

Kiev taken by Soviets, November 6.

Leningrad siege ends after 900 days, January 26, 1944.

Two German Corps encircled by Soviets west of Cherkassy, January 28.

German troops west of Cherkassy break out, leaving wounded and heavy equipment behind, February 15.

Soviet troops reach the River Dniester, March 17.

1st Panzer Army trapped then breaks out to the west, 28 March–7 April.

Crimea cleared of German troops, May 15.

Operation 'Bagration', the main Russian summer offensive begins, June 22.

Russian troops on outskirts of Warsaw suburbs, August 1.

Germans/Hungarians make a strong counter-attack in southern Carpathians but are repelled, September 5.

In battle for Belgrade, the city is taken by the Soviets, October 14–20.

Warsaw falls to the Soviets, January 17, 1945.

Battle for Budapest finally ends in Soviet victory, February 13.

Vienna falls to the Soviets, April 13.

Berlin surrenders to the Soviets, May 2.

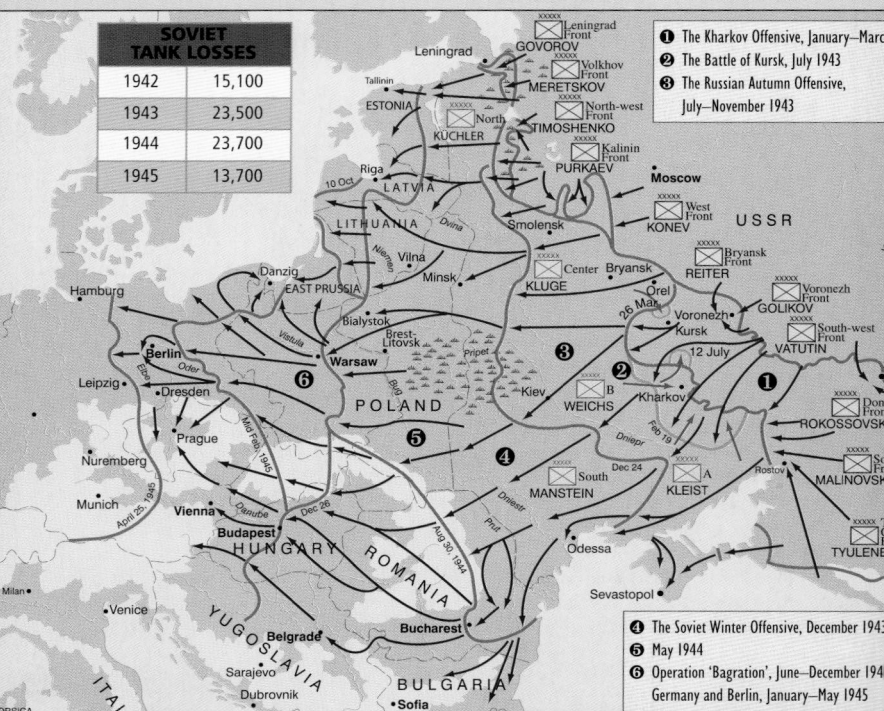

SOVIET TANK LOSSES	
1942	15,100
1943	23,500
1944	23,700
1945	13,700

❶ The Kharkov Offensive, January–March
❷ The Battle of Kursk, July 1943
❸ The Russian Autumn Offensive, July–November 1943

❹ The Soviet Winter Offensive, December 1943
❺ May 1944
❻ Operation 'Bagration', June–December 194
Germany and Berlin, January–May 1945

Leyte Gulf and the Philippines

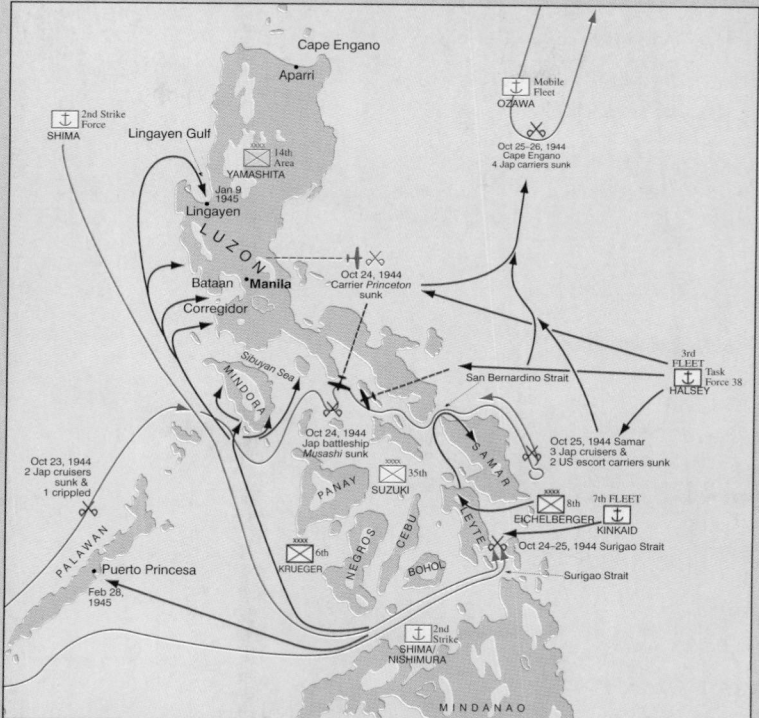

Battle for the Philippine Islands

begins: US Rangers land on Suluan Island, October 17, 1944.

US land on Leyte Island, October 20.

Naval Battle of Leyte Gulf, major defeat for the Japanese Navy, October 23–26.

US forces land on the island of Mindoro, December 15.

US forces land at Lingayen Gulf, Luzon, January 9, 1945.

US forces making slow progress because of the stiff resistance of the Japanese, January 16.

US forces land on west coast of Luzon, January 31.

US forces reach the outskirts of Manila, February 3.

Bataan peninsula secured by US forces, February 21.

PHILIPPINES

The American reconquest was the largest battle of the Pacific War

The campaign eliminated 450,000 Japanese troops

American casualties were 62,140, including 13,700 killed

US forces land on Corregidor, February 16.

X Corps lands on the island of Samar, February 19.

Corregidor secured, March 2.

Manila finally taken after a fierce battle which almost totally devastates the city, March 3.

Fighting continues until the very end of the war. The Japanese forces are cut off and slowly starved of supplies or reinforcements.

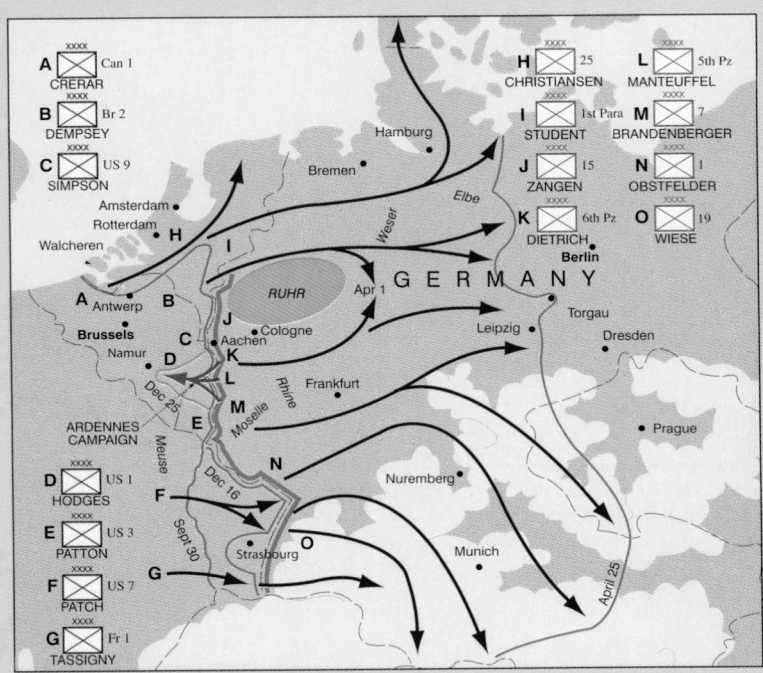

A Can 1 CRERAR
B Br 2 DEMPSEY
C US 9 SIMPSON
D US 1 HODGES
E US 3 PATTON
F US 7 PATCH
G Fr 1 TASSIGNY
H 25 CHRISTIANSEN
I 1st Para STUDENT
J 15 ZANGEN
K 6th Pz DIETRICH
L 5th Pz MANTEUFFEL
M 7 BRANDENBERGER
N 1 OBSTFELDER
O 19 WIESE

ARDENNES CAMPAIGN

German Ardennes offensive (Battle of the Bulge), December 16, 1944.

Germans surround Bastogne, December 22.

French First Army traps eight German divisions in Colmar pocket, January 20, 1945.

Allies eliminate the German salient, ending the German offensive in the Ardennes, January 28.

Battle of the Reichswald Forest, February 10.

US troops cross the River Roer, February 27.

Reichswald Forest cleared of German troops, March 4.

US troops seize the intact but damaged Rhine bridge at Remagen, March 7.

Remagen bridge finally collapses, March 17.

Patton's troops cross the Rhine at Oppenheim, March 22.

Montgomery's troops cross the Rhine at Emmerich and Rees, March 23.

British 6th Airborne Division and US 17th Airborne Division drop near Wesel east of the River Rhine, March 24.

US forces link up at Giessen, trapping the German LXXXIX Corps, March 28.

US forces encircle the German Army Group B in the 'Ruhr Pocket', trapping 325,000 troops, April 1.

US and Soviet troops meet at the River Elbe at Torgau, April 25.

German forces in north-west Germany surrender to Montgomery at Lüneburg Heath, May 4.

German forces surrender to Eisenhower at Reims, May 7.

'VE Day', Victory in Europe, the formal surrender of German forces, May 8.

Iwo Jima and Okinawa

US Marines land on Iwo Jima, initially meeting no resistance, but once ashore resistance is very intense, February 19, 1945.

Marines capture first airfield, February 20.

Mount Suribachi taken, February 23.

Second airfield taken, February 28.

Japanese hill positions taken after very fierce fighting, March 3.

US B-29 bombers land at Iwo Jima, March 4.

'The Meat Grinder' and the 'Bloody Gorge' positions are taken, March 10–11.

Marines reach the northern tip of the island, March 25.

Final *Banzai* charge by the Japanese defenders of Iwo Jima, March 26.

US forces land on the west coast of the Japanese island of Okinawa, April 1.

US forces reach the east coast, thus cutting the island in two, April 4.

First Mustang fighters operate from Iwo Jima, escorting B-29 bombers attacking Japan, April 7.

Formidable defensive lines in the south based on Shuri castle are attacked by the US, April 9.

Massive counter-attacks launched by Japanese are repulsed, May 4.

US forces breach the Shuri line and the Japanese fall back to the Oroka peninsula, May 18.

Motobura peninsula cleared by US Marines, April 20.

Naha, the capital city of Okinawa, captured by US forces, May 27.

Shuri castle taken by the Marines, May 29.

Marines take the Oroka peninsula, June 4.

Japanese start to surrender rather than fight to the end, June 19.

The end of the battle for Okinawa is marked by the suicide of the Japanese commanding officer, General Ushijima, June 22.

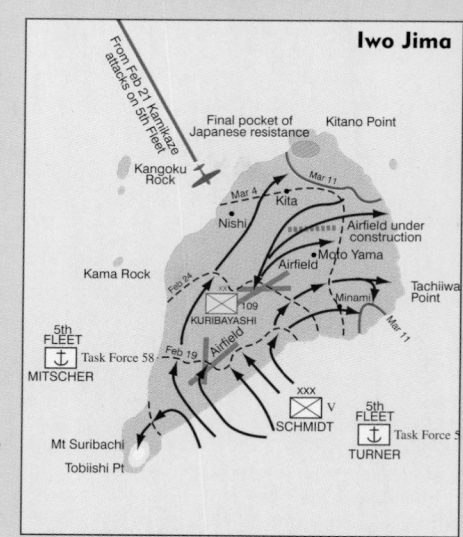

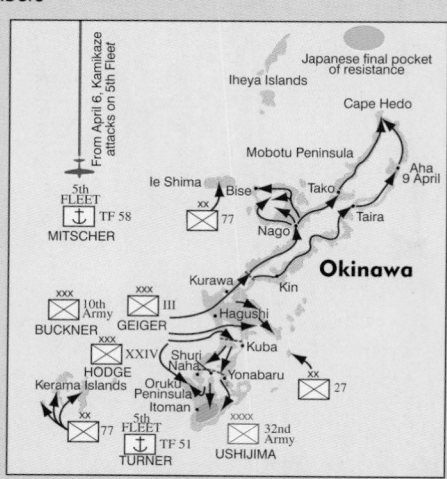

6 Civilians at War

Victory was made possible by the Allies' industrial superiority, particularly that of the United States, which possessed the necessary raw materials, skilled manpower and industries. In the USA there was a massive increase in food production, of which 10% was exported to allies through Lend-Lease. There was rationing, but the US civilians ate more, and better, than they did before the war. In the factories there was a huge increase in employment and production, which caused many families to move from small towns and rural areas to the big industrial cities. The average working week rose from 38 hours to 47. Productivity increases were dramatic: for example, it took only a third as many work hours to build a ship in 1945 as it did in 1943. There was a huge increase in the number of women working in heavy industry, replacing the men in the workforce.

British women played a very important part in the war effort, replacing many of the men who normally worked in the factories and heavy industry. In Britain, blackouts were enforced immediately and children evacuated. During the *Blitz* many British cities were bombed, starting with London in early September 1940. During one period London was bombed for two and a half months continuously, night after night. The people had to contend with austerity, strict rationing and bombing, but in general the British stoicism shone through and civilian morale remained high. British democracy carried on, and by-elections continued to be held. British men and women were directed to work in any industry that was thought necessary by the government. Young men often were conscripted to work in the coal mines as opposed to military service.

In Germany, in the early years of the war, domestic rationing was not at first introduced, but as the war progressed it became necessary, although civilian morale remained high. In the German-occupied countries, food was seized and shipped back to the German people. The Nazis resisted the need for women to undertake compulsory work

American female shipyard welders

Londoners sheltering in the London Underground during the Blitz

service for ideological reasons. Instead, women were paid a generous allowance by the state to stay at home and have babies. The Nazi state outlawed listening to any foreign radio stations. Any criticism of the state was an offence, and many offences were punishable by death. At first the bombing of German population centres was light, but it became increasingly intense and by the time the Americans entered the war, alongside RAF Bomber Command, city after city was devastated, culminating in the horrific raid on Dresden at the end of the war.

When the Germans invaded the USSR the Council for Evacuation proved essential for Soviet survival, in particular for the women and children. Over 16 million people were evacuated by the Council plus 10 million refugees. Many people went east to the factories and steelworks constructed in the Urals and beyond, to build the weapons to win the war. Some areas of the Soviet Union did welcome the Germans, initially as

liberators from the sufferings under Stalin, but this was unfounded optimism. Life for the Soviet citizen was very hard, and the people suffered from every form of privation.

The Japanese people found that gradual changes in normal civilian life were being made. From 1939 controls were placed on daily necessities which became more and more severe as the conflict progressed. Military priorities started to dominate life. All group travel began to be forbidden. Education was reduced, and limits on working hours of women and children were waived. Then American bombers started to attack Japan's towns and cities in earnest and hundreds of thousands of people were killed in the bombing and incendiary raids. By 1945 Japan's economy and society were starting to come apart. The US naval blockade caused severe raw material and food shortages. After the two atomic bomb raids and the surrender, on September 2, 1945, Japanese society was physically and mentally disarmed.

6 Refugees

In Poland, as soon as the war began, some civilians fled from the combat zones, and from the enemy, to safer areas. In Belgium and France, this trickle become a flood, often jamming the roads and handicapping the advancing Allied troops as they moved forward to meet the Germans. To amplify the confusion and terror for the *Blitzkrieg*, the Luftwaffe would sometimes machine-gun the columns of refugees, causing even more disorder for the Allied troops.

In the USSR, where the state had plans for evacuation, large numbers of refugees fled spontaneously, clogging up the transport systems, thus interfering with Soviet troop movements. There were, possibly, 10 million plus 16 million official evacuees.

During the winter of 1944–45 the Allies were gradually closing in on Germany. Millions of German people began to flee, especially from the advancing Communist troops. The German rail and road system had been disrupted by bombing and the German state machinery was disintegrating; some areas were close to anarchy. The number of refugees in Europe from this period can only be estimated, but the figure has been put at 30 million.

With the collapse of the Third Reich, millions of displaced people, mostly those who had been made to work as forced labour under the Germans, criss-crossed Europe, often on foot, trying to make their way to what remained of their homes and their families.

Resistance Movements

6

TOTAL WAR

Every country occupied by the Axis formed resistance movements against their occupation. There were two forms of resistance, passive and active.

Passive, non-violent acts, on their own could not dislodge a determined occupying power but they sometimes did save lives, modify the occupying forces' policies and assist Allied military operations.

The Netherlands offered mostly passive resistance and because it did have an effect the Germans took very harsh reprisals against the people.

In October 1943, after a tip-off from a German attaché, the Danish resistance organised the escape to neutral Sweden of most of their Jewish population, who otherwise were to be arrested. In Berlin, attempts to deport Jews who were married to non-Jews met with spontaneous opposition and the deportations were stopped. In Bulgaria, mass opposition forced the Jewish deportations to be halted.

Railway workers across Europe organised go-slows at critical times during the war. For example, during the summer of 1944 the general attitude of non-cooperation seriously limited the availability of the railway system of France to the German Army at the time of the Normandy landings.

Active resistance included such policies as killing and sabotage. Several Allied secret services, for example the British SOE and the American OSS, often assisted in providing arms, explosives or specialist equipment.

The French resistance, the *Maquis* (literally, 'scrub') centred on the River Rhône, did not really become active until 1942. It was politically divided between the Communists and the Gaullists. When the Allies landed in France in 1944 it assisted the Allied troops. On August 19, 1944 the *Maquis* rose against the German occupation forces in Paris. Six days later the city fell to the troops of the Free French Army.

The Polish resistance warned the British of the development of the V-2 rocket and even managed to smuggle

Jewish prisoners during the uprising of the Warsaw Ghetto, Poland, 1943

Resistance Movements

Paris resists

a sample engine to England. There were two Warsaw uprisings. The first was in April–May 1943 by the Jews in the Ghetto established there by the Germans. Even though inspired, it was crushed. The second uprising began on August 1, 1944, the resistance movement hoping that the Russians would come to its aid. It lasted for two months and the Russians, who were on the outskirts of the city, did not attempt to help. The Germans crushed the rising and 250,000 Poles died.

German forces occupied parts of Italy when the country signed an armistice with the Allies. Many Italian soldiers in the occupied areas resisted, most groups being organised by the Communists. By the spring of 1944 their numbers in the mountains were in the region of 100,000. During the summer of that year the Nazis unleashed a terrible offensive upon them and the resistance forces were devastated. Their final act was the capture and execution of Mussolini.

The mountains of Yugoslavia were perfect for guerrilla operations. There were two groups, the Çetniks and the Communists under Tito but these did not operate in unison and eventually ended up fighting each other. The Communists won and Tito became the leader of that country.

In Czechoslovakia, the resistance was made up of many groups. One group of exiles, flown in from London, assassinated Reinhard Heydrich, the *Reichsprotektor* and second most powerful man in the SS.

Norwegian resistance was mostly passive, but in November 1942 they helped to destroy the Germans' heavy water plant vital to the production of a nuclear weapon. This set the German nuclear programme back by two years.

In the USSR, the partisans operated behind enemy lines, gathering intelligence and disrupting the German lines of communication. This type of warfare became very brutal, neither side paying any attention to suffering caused to the local people, and no quarter was given by either side.

Atrocities 6

The list of atrocities committed during the war is large and, sadly, many of the perpetrators were never punished. Typical was the massacre in the French village of Oradour-sur-Glane in June 1944 by the German 2nd Waffen SS Panzer Division. It was carried out in revenge for local resistance activity. The Germans herded all the villagers, men, women and children, into some barns and the village church and then set the buildings alight. As people tried to flee they were shot down. A few did manage to escape. The Germans then looted and burned the village. Oradour-sur-Glane now stands, unoccupied, as a memorial.

In 1942 the Czech village of Lidice was razed to the ground, the 198 men of the village were shot and the 293 women and children were abducted or imprisoned in reprisal for the assassination of the top-ranking SS man Rienhard Heydrich. In the Soviet Union and Greece the burning of villages was a routine reprisal after any sabotage incident. In late March and early April 1945, 250 Dutchmen were killed in retaliation for the death of another senior SS officer who was accidentally shot. In October 1941,

3,000 innocent Yugoslavs were killed over a two-day period, in retaliation for attacks made on the occupying forces.

As a matter of course, German Waffen SS units did not take military prisoners. In France in May 1940, soldiers of the British Royal Norfolk Regiment were captured by the Germans. They were then lined up against a farmhouse wall and shot. The 97 soldiers were murdered by troops of the 2nd SS Totenkopf (Death's Head) Regiment. In 1944, at Malmédy in Belgium, SS troops shot 129 US prisoners, 86 of whom died.

Atrocities occurred on both sides. In Sicily, at Biscari, in the summer of 1943, 74 Italian and two German prisoners were shot by US troops. There is a documented account of Japanese prisoners being marched into the jungle and massacred by vengeful Borneo tribesmen as their Australian captors looked on.

The Japanese believed surrender was shameful and often shot their prisoners. When Japanese troops captured the Chinese city of Nanking, and during what is referred to as the 'Rape of Nanking', between 200,000 and 300,000 people were slaughtered.

The Holocaust

Twelve million people died in the Nazi concentration camps, of whom some 6,000,000 were Jewish. The others included gypsies, homosexuals, the mentally or physically ill and people whom, for whatever reason, the Nazis considered enemies of the German state.

A Jew was defined by the Germans in the Nuremberg Laws of 1935 as being someone with one Jewish grandparent. A quarter of the German Jews were eventually killed. Many fled before the war, many making their way to other European countries and often finding themselves back under Nazi power when that country was conquered by the Germans.

In Poland, between September and October 1939, 3,000 Jews were among more than 10,000 Polish civilians who were shot in the streets. In Russia, the shootings continued in the fields and ditches as curious bystanders stood and watched. In Kiev, for example, 33,000 Jewish men, women and children were killed in just three days. The Germans also created ghettos for the Jews, where they were confined and where many starved to death or died of disease.

By 1941 the Germans had built extermination camps specifically for

ESTIMATED NUMBERS OF JEWS MURDERED, BY NATIONALITY	
Poland	3,000,000
USSR	1,000,000
Romania	470,000
Czechoslovakia	277,000
Hungary	200,000
Germany	160,000
Lithuania	140,000
The Netherlands	106,000
France	83,000
Latvia	80,000
Greece	69,000
Yugoslavia	67,000
Austria	65,000
Belgium	24,000
Italy	8,000
Estonia	1,000
Norway	728
Luxembourg	700
Libya	562
Denmark	77
Finland	15

the purposes of mass murder by gassing. Many Jews were also worked or beaten to death in factories or the camps that were attached. At one of the biggest camps, Auschwitz-Birkenau in Poland, trains brought victims from all over occupied Europe who were then murdered on an industrial scale. It is estimated that between 1¼ and 1½ million died in this camp alone, including 800,000 Jews.

Approximately 50,000,000 people died as a consequence of World War II, although the precise number will never be known. The USSR paid the highest price by far in terms of people who lost their lives, 50% of whom were civilians.

Of the total, the military made up approximately 22,000,000 of the war-related deaths. Of the remaining 28,000,000, 12,000,000 died in the concentration camps and 1,500,000 directly from aerial bombing. The remaining 14,500,000 died from other war-related causes, of which some 7,500,000 were in China. It is estimated that 1,000,000 German refugees died during the winter and spring of 1944–45 as they fled from the advancing Soviet armies.

In Bengal, India, during the period 1943–46, between 3,500,000 and 3,800,000 people may have died as a result of famine and the epidemic diseases that accompanied it. It was caused indirectly by the fall of Burma in 1942 and the consequent increase in local food prices. This figure has not been included in the table opposite.

APPROXIMATE NUMBERS KILLED, BY COUNTRY	
Albania	20,000
Australia	27,000
Austria	310,000
Belgium	100,000
Bulgaria	17,000
Brazil	1,200
Canada	42,000
China	10,500,000
Czechoslovakia	350,000
Denmark	7,000
Estonia	80,000
Finland	90,000
France	600,000
Germany	5,500,000
Greece	250,000
Hungary	400,000
India	36,000
Italy	300,000
Japan	2,300,000
Latvia	200,000
Lithuania	300,000
Luxembourg	7,000
The Netherlands	200,000
New Zealand	12,000
Norway	10,000
The Philippines	120,000
Poland	5,800,000
Romania	500,000
South Africa	9,000
UK	362,000
USA	409,000
USSR	20,000,000
Yugoslavia	1,500,000

6 War Crimes and Trials

President Roosevelt was aware that war crimes were being committed by the Axis powers and warned them of this fact and that they would be brought to justice. These crimes were mainly concerned with breaches of the Geneva and Hague Conventions. The London Charter of the International Military Tribunal, August 8, 1945, was established to try the major war criminals, who would be tried for crimes against peace (waging a war of aggression), war crimes (violations of the laws and customs of war) and crimes against humanity (inhumanity and the persecution of civilians).

The list of people to be tried contained 24 Germans, including Göring, Dönitz, Hess and Speer. Between November 20, 1945 and October 1, 1946 the Nuremberg Trials were held. Eleven of the defendants were sentenced to hanging, three received life sentences, two 20 years, one 15 years and one 10 years and three were acquitted. Göring, who was sentenced to death, committed suicide before his execution.

An International War Tribunal was also set up to try 28 leading Japanese for war crimes. The Tokyo War Crimes trials were held between May 3, 1946 and November 6, 1948. The most prominent defendant was General Tojo. By the conclusion of the trial two defendants had died, one had been found to be mentally unfit, and the rest found guilty. Seven, including Tojo, were sentenced to hang, sixteen to life imprisonment, one to 20 years and one to seven years.

In the Far East over 2,000 regional trials were held by the USA, Britain, Canada, France, the Netherlands and the Philippines, and these continued until 1951. The majority of indictments were for the maltreatment and murder of prisoners of war and civilians. The high number of convictions arose from the fact that, for example, 4% of Anglo-American POWs died in German prison camps while 27% died in Japanese camps. Overall 5,700 were indicted, some 3,000 of whom were convicted, and imprisoned for varying terms, and 920 were sentenced to death.

The Nuremberg Trials, with the defendants in the dock

This selection lists the principal military museums in the country featuring exhibits, artefacts and material concerning World War II. In addition, there are many excellent regimental museums.

100th Bomb Group Association, Common Road, Dickleburgh, Diss, Norfolk, IP21 4PH.
www.aeroflight.co.uk/mus

Cabinet War Rooms, Clive Steps King Charles Street, London, SW1A 2AQ
cwr.iwm.org.uk

East England Tank Museum, Elveden Road, Barnham, Thetford, Suffolk, IP24 2SY
www.tankmuseum.com

Firepower, The Royal Artillery, Museum, Royal Arsenal, Woolwich, London, SE18 6ST
www.firepower.org.uk

Fleet Air Arm Museum, Box D6, RNAS Yeovilton, Near Ilchester, Somerset, BA22 8HT
www.fleetairarm.com

HMS Belfast, Morgan's Lane Tooley Street, London SE1 2JH
hmsbelfast.iwm.org.uk

Imperial War Museum, Duxford, Cambridgeshire, CB2 4QR
duxford.iwm.org.uk

Imperial War Museum, Lambeth Road, London, SE1 6HZ
london.iwm.org.uk

Imperial War Museum North, The Quays, Trafford Wharf, Trafford Park, Manchester, M17 1TE
north.iwm.org.uk

Lashenden Air Warfare Museum, Headcorn Aerodrome, Headcorn, Ashford, Kent, TN27 9HX,
www.tigerclub.co.uk

Muckleburgh Collection, Weybourne Camp, Weybourne, Norfolk, NR25 7EG
www.muckleburgh.co.uk

National Army Museum, Royal Hospital Road, Chelsea, London, SW3 4HT
www.national-army-museum.ac.uk

Parachute Regiment And Airborne Forces Museum, Browning Barracks, Aldershot, Hampshire, GU11 2BU
www.parachute-regiment.com/museum

RAF Museum Cosford, Royal Air Force Museum, Cosford, Shifnal Shropshire, TF11 8UP
www.rafmuseum.org.uk/cosford

REME Museum, Isaac Newton Road, Arborfield, Berkshire RG2 9NJ,
www.rememuseum.org.uk

Royal Air Force Museum London, Grahame Park Way, London, NW9 5LL
www.rafmuseum.org.uk/london

The Royal Engineers, Museum of Military Engineering, Prince Arthur Road, Gillingham, Kent, ME4 4UG
www.army.mod.uk/royalengineers/museum

Royal Marines Museum, Southsea, Hampshire, PO4 9PX
www.royalmarinesmuseum.co.uk

Royal Navy Museum, HM Naval Base, (PP66), Portsmouth, Hampshire. PO1 3NH
www.royalnavalmuseum.org

Royal Navy Submarine Museum, Haslar Road, Gosport, Hampshire, PO12 2AS
www.rnsubmus.co.uk

The Tank Museum, Bovington, Dorset, BH20 6JG.
www.tankmuseum.co.uk

Spitfire and Hurricane Memorial, The Airfield, Manston Road, Ramsgate, Kent, CT12 5DF,
www.spitfire-museum.com

Further Reading

Beevor, Antony, *Berlin: The Downfall, 1945*, 2002
— *Stalingrad*, 1998
Brown, David, *Warship Losses of World War Two*, 1990
Burt, R. A., *British Battleships 1919–1939*, 1993
Calvocoressi, Peter, and Guy Wint, *Total War*, 1972
Chamberlain, Peter, and Chris Ellis, *British and American Tanks of World War II*, 1969
— *Pictorial History of Tanks of the World 1915–45*, 1972
Chamberlain, Peter, Hilary L. Doyle and Thomas L. Jentz, *The Encyclopedia of German Tanks of World War Two*, 1978
Chambers, John Whiteclay, *The Oxford Companion to American Military History*, 1999
Chronicle of the Second World War (1990), reissued as *World War II Day by Day*, 2001
Chronology and Index of the Second World War, Royal Institute of International Affairs, 1975
Costello, John, and Terry Hughes, *The Battle of the Atlantic*, 1977
— *The Pacific War*, 1981
Cressman, Robert J., The Official *Chronology of the U.S. Navy in World War II*, 1999
Davidson, Edward, and Dale Manning, *Chronology of World War Two*, 1999
Davis, Brian L., *German Army Uniforms and Insignia, 1933–1945*, 1971
— *Uniforms and Insignia of the Luftwaffe*, 2 vols, 1991, 1995
Dear, Ian, and M. R. D. Foot, *The Oxford Companion to the Second World War*, 1995
Delaney, John, *The Blitzkrieg Campaigns*, 1996
Delve, Ken, and Peter Jacobs, *The Six-Year Offensive: Bomber Command in World War Two*, 1992
Ellis, John, *The World War II Databook*, 1993
Ethell Jeffrey, L., and David C. Isby, *G.I. Victory: The U.S. Army in World War II in Color*, 1995
Freeman, Roger A., *The Mighty Eighth*, 1970
Gilbert, Martin, *The Day the War Ended: VE-Day 1945 in Europe and Around the World*, 2004
— *Holocaust: A History of the Jews of Europe during the Second World War*, 1987
— *Second World War: A Complete History*, 2004
Goralski, Robert, *World War II Almanac, 1931–1945*, 1981
Hastings, Max, *Armageddon: The Battle for Germany, 1944–1945*, 2004
— *Bomber Command*, 1979
— *Overlord: D-Day and the Battle for Normandy, 1944*, 1999
Hogg, Ian V., *British and American Artillery of World War 2*, 1978
— and John Weeks, *Military Small Arms of the 20th Century*, 1991
Irving, David, *The Rise and Fall of the Luftwaffe*, 1973
Jackson, W. G. F., *The Battle for Italy*, 1967
Jentschura, Hansgeorg, Dieter Jung and Peter Mickel, *Warships of the Imperial Japanese Navy, 1869–1945*, 1970, English trans. 1977
Johnson, Brian, *The Secret War*, 1978
Jones, R. V., *Most Secret War*, 1978
Keegan, John (ed), *Churchill's Generals*, 1991
— *The Times Atlas of the Second World War*, 1989
— *Who Was Who in World War II*, 1978
Kemp, Paul, *U-Boats Destroyed*, 1997
Kershaw, Ian, *Making Friends with Hitler: Lord Londonderry, the Nazis and the Road to World War II*, 2004
Latimer, John, *Burma: The Forgotten War*, 2004
Lewin, Ronald, *Ultra Goes to War*, 1978
Macksey, Kenneth, *Rommel: Battles and Campaigns*, 1979
Messenger, Charles, *World War Two Chronological Atlas*, 1989
Pimlott, John, *The Viking Atlas of World War II*, 1995
Pitt, Barrie and Frances, *The Chronological Atlas of World War II*, 1989
Price, Alfred, *Instruments of Darkness*, 1967
Rohwer, Jürgen, and Gerhard Hümmelchen, *Chronology of the War at Sea, 1939–1945*, 1972, 1974, 1992
Rooney, David, *Wingate and the Chindits*, 1994
Rössler, Eberhard, *The U-Boat*, 1975, English trans. 1981
Shulman, Milton, *Defeat in the West*, 2004
Tarrant, V. E., *The U-Boat Offensive 1914–1945*, 1989
Weal, Elke C. and John A., and Richard F. Barker, *Combat Aircraft of World War Two*, 1977
Whitley, M. J., *Battleships of World War Two*, 1998
— *Cruisers of World War Two*, 1995
— *Destroyers of World War Two*, 1988
— *German Capital Ships of World War Two*, 1989

The place of publication in almost all cases is London and/or New York.